Taunton's

NEW Bathroom
IDEA BOOK

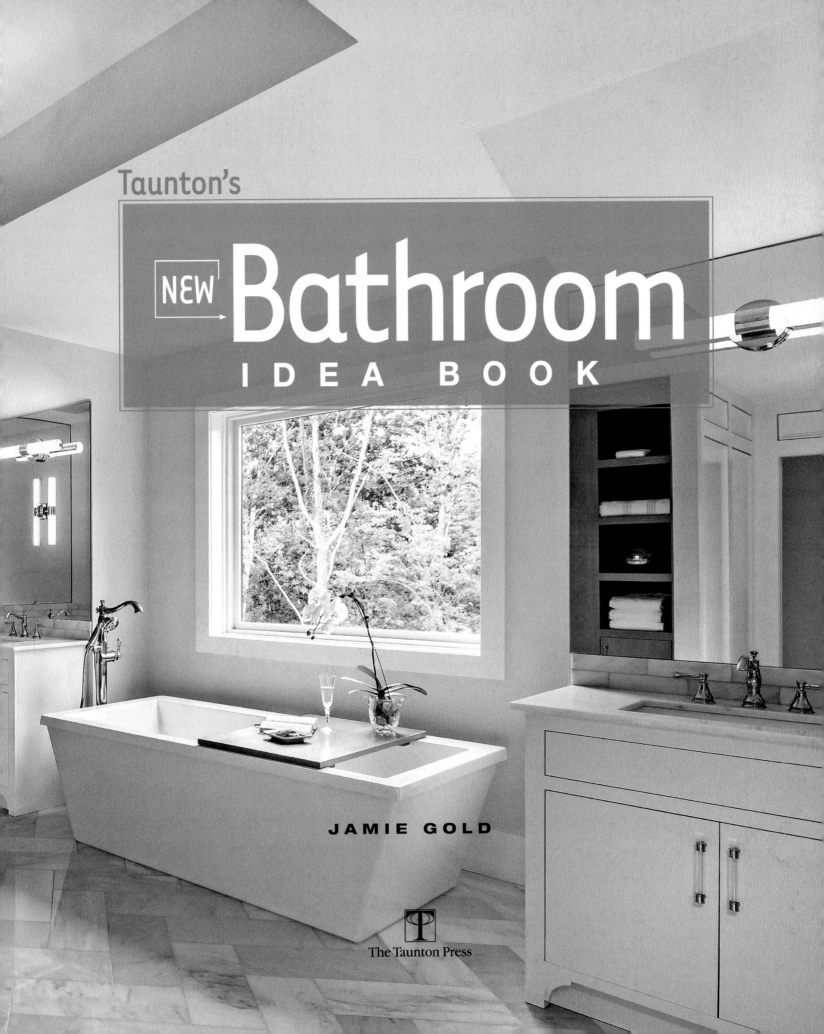

Taunton's

New Bathroom
IDEA BOOK

JAMIE GOLD

The Taunton Press

The Taunton Press
Inspiration for hands-on living®

The Taunton Press, Inc.
63 South Main Street, PO Box 5506
Newtown, CT 06470-5506
e-mail: tp@taunton.com

Editors: Christina Glennon and Peter Chapman
Copy Editor: Nina Rynd Whitnah
Jacket/Cover design: Kim Adis
Interior design: Kim Adis
Layout: Alison Wilkes
Illustrator: Jean Tuttle
Photo Editor: Katy Binder
Front cover photographers: (center and bottom right photos) Mark Lohman;
(top right photo) courtesy of Brizo (www.brizo.com)
Back cover photographers: (top right photo) Susan Teare; (center right photo)
Mark Lohman; (bottom left photo) Eric Roth; (bottom right photo) courtesy of
Brizo (www.brizo.com)

Library of Congress Cataloging-in-Publication Data

Names: Gold, Jamie, 1960- author.
Title: Taunton's new bathroom idea book / Jamie Gold.
Other titles: New bathroom idea book
Description: Newtown, CT : The Taunton Press, Inc., 2017.
Identifiers: LCCN 2016056526 | ISBN 9781631864056
Subjects: LCSH: Bathrooms. | Interior decoration.
Classification: LCC NK2117.B33 G65 2017 | DDC 747.7/8--dc23
LC record available at https://lccn.loc.gov/2016056526

The following names/manufacturers appearing in *New Bathroom Idea Book*
are trademarks: Bluetooth®, Corian®, WaterSense®.

Printed in the United States of America
10 9 8 7 6 5 4 3 2

Dedication

This book is dedicated to my wonderful, incredibly talented father who gave me a strong appreciation for well-crafted spaces as I was growing up and who continues to give me so much love and support all these decades later.

acknowledgments

Writing this second book for The Taunton Press has been a terrific experience, and I'm so grateful to so many people for their guidance and support in bringing it to print.

I am particularly thankful for my publishing colleagues, including Rosalind Loeb Wanke, Katy Binder, Lynne Phillips, Sharon Zagata, Nina Whitnah, and, most of all, my tireless editors, Christina Glennon, who gave birth to a baby while also giving birth to this book, and Peter Chapman.

The *New Bathroom Idea Book* would be much shorter and far less beautiful without the brilliant designers, architects, and builders who let us photograph their projects for publication. These include Cheryl Kees Clendenon, Julia Kleyman, Anne Kellett, Jeffrey Hellmuth, Aparna Vijayan, Jill S. Jarrett, Lauren Villano, Tony Garcia, Paul Davis, Brad Rabinowitz, and Mitra Samimi-Urich.

In addition to the above-named professionals, I am incredibly grateful to their representatives, their clients who let us into their homes, and to the talented photographers who expertly captured these handsome spaces. I am also grateful to the many designers who supplied photographs of bathrooms they had created, and to the countless industry professionals who supplied two years' worth of photographs from their manufacturer, association, and retailer connections, sometimes in response to urgent eleventh-hour emails.

I also need to thank the following colleagues who generously shared their specialized insights with me: Bob Borson, Jennifer Ho, Roger Larrison, Diane Williams, Amy Gil, Sheen Fischer, Ryan Fasan, Nadja Pentic, Dean Larkin, Vicky Lodge, David Van Wert, and Tyler Tremble.

My authorship of this book would not have been possible without my industry friends who have been so supportive since I became a kitchen and bath designer in 2004. I would particularly like to thank Terry Smith for being the best Southern California project partner a designer could have, Nadja Pentic (again!) for being a phenomenal Northern California project partner, and Sherrie Pantalon for her tremendous help in earning my CKD (Certified Kitchen Designer) credential.

On the personal side, I couldn't be more grateful for having such amazing friends, family, and coaches. While I'm not a professional athlete and never expect to become one, I could not spend the hours necessary to create a book like this without stepping away from the desk for a mile or 26! Thank you to my many trainers, both paid and volunteer, for your time, insights, and support.

contents

introduction   2

plan your bath   4

work with your space   30

find your style   52

fixtures and faucets   72

the shower space   102

storage   126

floors, walls, windows, and doors   148

light, heat, and ventilation   170

entertainment, electronics, and extras   184

decorative touches   192

photo credits   214

introduction

I GREW UP IN A THREE-STORY HOME with only one full bathroom. My parents, brother, sister, and I all shared that basic 5 by 8 space down the hall from our upstairs bedrooms. I've often wondered since becoming a kitchen and bath designer whether later owners created a master suite to give themselves privacy. I could probably find out with an Internet search if I tried, but that would mean accepting that the pretty red and white bedroom in which I slept, dreamed, kissed rock star posters good night, and finished my homework until I was 16 no longer exists. My bedroom was next to my parents' room and directly upstairs from a half bath, making it the likely space to become a new en suite master bath.

Homeowners across the country wrestle with issues like these to meet the needs of privacy, water conservation, and growing households. Do you settle for one less bedroom, add on to the size of your house,

steal a closet to expand, or change the footprint of an existing bathroom for better storage and traffic flow? What are the issues involved with making such changes?

There are more options than ever today to meet evolving needs. New manufacturing processes have made water and energy conservation easier and more pleasant, even as our busy lives demand spa-like comforts from our bathrooms. As many downsize their homes to free up funds for travel and hobbies, storage gets smarter with interior accessories to optimize compact spaces. And as we get more and more attached to our electronic devices, even our bathrooms give us new connectivity options.

The Hot Trends sections in each chapter cover some of the smartest, most useful advances in the bathroom industry in recent years—like digital showering systems that preset your preferences, and medicine cabinets with built-in speakers and chargers

for your tablets and phones. All 10 Hot Trends were included to help you plan smarter and choose from the most useful ideas and innovations for your bathrooms. In these pages, you'll find both new approaches to planning your space and new resources for equipping it.

Not everything in your new bathroom needs to be completely new either. So many remodels preserve existing elements like flooring, vanities, or fixtures—or they phase in new ones over time, as need and budgets dictate. For projects like these, I've included Bathroom Redo & Reuse sections in each chapter. These are designed to help you update your bathroom in a way that makes sense for that space and for any related rooms. This is especially crucial for a master suite, but also benefits bathrooms that tie into your entertaining spaces, like powder rooms.

So as you plan an entirely new—or just newly improved—bathroom, you'll have

the best information available to guide you through the process, as well as tips proven in hundreds of projects completed over the years. My most important role as an independent kitchen and bath designer is making the remodeling process as straightforward, well informed, and smooth as possible. As I travel to trade shows around the world, I'm constantly on the lookout for new products and ideas that make my clients' lives easier and durable, low-maintenance materials that can add style to their homes.

My role as author, design blogger, and journalist is the same. I want to guide you through the best choices for your home and family. This is equally true for the reader investing a hundred dollars in a new WaterSense faucet...or a hundred thousand in a new master suite. Adding or updating a bathroom is an investment in your home. The *New Bathroom Idea Book* is an investment in achieving your best outcome.

plan your bath

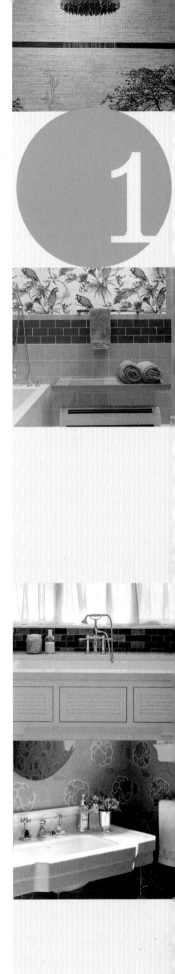

● ● ●

THE MODERN AMERICAN BATHROOM CAME INTO BEING TWO CENTURIES ago, but it was pretty primitive. Your grandparents or great-grandparents may still recall a time when they didn't have indoor plumbing. In fact, there are still U.S. houses that lack interior bathrooms.

Homes today typically have at least one bathroom with a toilet, sink, and tub or shower. This became the norm in major U.S. cities and the suburbs that boomed after World War II. Many of those modest dwellings had only one bathroom shared by the entire household. As homes began growing larger in the prosperous decades following the war, master bathrooms for the homeowners became standard in new homes.

Secondary baths were created for the family's children, grandparents, and overnight guests as American houses continued to grow from their 1960s 1,200-square-foot average to the over 3,000-square-foot suburban homes of the McMansion era.

Bathroom counts increased as homes grew, and so did the size of master baths. Specialized bathrooms, like the pool bath and powder room, also started showing up as houses grew larger.

The need for water conservation has also increased. Toilets, showerheads, and sink faucets are all available now with lower usage rates, often mandated by local codes.

The master bath is a relatively new phenomenon in American homes. This one exemplifies modern style to match its urban setting with a freestanding tub and wet room layout. Even the minimalist shower enclosure and uncovered windows emphasize contemporary style.

assess your needs

● ● ● BATHROOM PROJECTS HAPPEN FOR MANY different reasons. The key to successfully completing one is to be clear about your goals before you start. Did your household grow in size? Did an aging parent move in with the family? Is the home's sole bathroom getting too much traffic in the morning?

Make a list, itemizing the shortcomings of your existing space if you're remodeling or the needs for your new space if you are adding a bathroom. Think in terms of both the bathroom's users and the space you're working with.

Assessing a bathroom's needs includes considering storage requirements (e.g., curling iron, hair dryer, cosmetics, dental hygiene supplies, etc.); any accessibility requirements for users of the space (e.g., a shower they can roll a wheelchair into); and usage patterns not being accommodated by the existing space (e.g., two users on the same school or work schedule with only one sink).

Many bathrooms are enhanced by the addition of a double vanity and two sinks. This setup can ease traffic flow if a couple gets ready together, and it provides storage for each person's toiletries. A floating vanity delivers all of that capacity while adding less visual bulk to the room.

BELOW Bathrooms often have to accommodate additional items, like towels and extra bath tissue, that don't fit into a vanity. Storage towers with open and closed sections can meet those needs. Open areas are ideal for displaying attractive towels or baskets, while opaque glass or drawers can conceal bulk necessities.

ABOVE Toilet area cabinets can provide additional storage capacity in a bathroom. They are often used to store personal items out of sight. They can be installed at the same time to match the vanity, or added later to coordinate if increased capacity is needed.

assess your space

● ● ● IF YOUR PROJECT IS A REMODEL OF AN existing bathroom, you will either be looking at the current space or a combination of current and potential space you can "steal" from an adjacent room to increase your bathroom's size. If, for example, you want to take your master from a tub-shower combination to separate shower and tub, it's rare that you'll be able to accomplish this change without breaking a wall.

If you're looking to add an entirely new bathroom to your house, the first questions to consider are what purpose will it serve, where does it need to be located, does the home need to be expanded to accommodate it, and what type of professionals, budget, and permitting are required to complete the project.

If one of your remodeling objectives is creating an oversize master shower like the one shown here, you'll need to decide which elements are most important to each user. Should it have steam, a bench, multiple showerheads? If so, you might need to take space from an adjacent room or closet.

ABOVE This bathroom project added a separate tub, which isn't always possible in an existing footprint. Sometimes, space can be borrowed from an adjacent room to make the inclusion of both possible.

LEFT Many homeowners today opt for an enhanced shower in place of a tub. Enhancements can include features like rain showerheads that add a luxurious experience, while still using less water than a soaking tub.

face-lift or full remodel

●●● AFTER YOU'VE ASSESSED YOUR NEEDS, you'll have a better idea of how your current space is meeting them. If accessibility is an issue, or if the current layout is creating traffic jams five mornings a week, your bathroom needs more than a face-lift. It will need a full or partial remodel. This entails replacing fixtures and cabinetry, as well as potentially altering the layout to accommodate more storage or better accessibility.

If, on the other hand, the countertop is a jumble of items that don't fit in the vanity, the medicine cabinet is chipped, the lighting is poor, and the shower curtain hasn't been changed since the new millennium, you may be able to just add some storage elements and style improvements.

Knowing the scope of your project early on will help you determine which professionals are best suited to the job and how much time and investment are required.

Full remodels typically cost thousands of dollars and require months of time and work planning, designing, and constructing them. They involve professionals, purchase orders, and contracts. Face-lifts can usually be done in a series of weekends, either by a skilled do-it-yourselfer, specialized trade professional, or handyman. Depending upon the update list and your own skills, you may be able to give the bathroom a face-lift for less than $1,000.

Consider the existing space you have available and whether it will work for your new goals. What elements—like vanities, countertops, and fixtures—make sense to keep or replace? These will help determine the scope of your project and which professional to hire.

ABOVE An existing vanity can be improved with the addition of accessories that increase storage capacity. Updated knobs, faucets, and lighting can easily enhance the look without major work or expense.

LEFT Creating a spacious new shower with multiple heads, niches, lighting, a bench, and grab bars requires extensive planning. A professional would usually be engaged to design such a space and tradespeople hired to install all of the elements, perhaps at the direction of a general contractor.

RENOVATE WHILE KEEPING YOUR
CABINETRY, TOILET, AND TUB

UPDATE HARDWARE

New hardware can really enhance the look of a cabinet. Choose styles whose lines and finish coordinate with each other and with your faucets, for the most pulled-together look. Keep in mind that a lever handle is easier to use than a knob, especially by wet or older hands.

CHANGE SIMPLER SURFACES

Wall color and floor tile are surfaces that can be more affordable to change than countertops, tubs, and shower surrounds. Remove dated wallpaper in favor of a fresh coat of paint. Swap out builder grade floor tile with a weekend's work. Both can be accomplished by knowledgeable do-it-yourselfers.

REMOVE VISUAL CLUTTER

Small details like moving a trash can out of sight and updating wall art can take a bathroom from basic to designer with a very minor investment of time and money.

TIME FOR A REDO?

ABOVE Changing fixtures can be expensive and isn't always necessary. You can improve a bathroom's style while leaving its tub, toilet, and sink in place, thus saving considerable time and money.

FAR LEFT, TOP The modern silver finish pull will dress up the vanity and tie into the shower door.

FAR LEFT, BOTTOM New floor tile can give a room a fresh new look. A neutral color will always work well, and gray adds a coolness that the space is currently lacking. This tile's new shape will update the room's style and add a designer element.

TOP LEFT A cabinet accessory gets an unsightly trash can off the floor and out of view. It is installed on the back of the vanity door, taking advantage of space that isn't being used. The new location may also be more convenient for a vanity user who doesn't want to toss trash over the toilet.

BOTTOM LEFT Replacing dated wallpaper with paint can easily freshen up a tired-looking space and is often a DIY-friendly project. The new color is deep, rich, and saturated, adding a cool elegance to the room.

A well-planned bath will address storage, lighting, and privacy needs while incorporating stylish details.

develop your budget

●●● ONCE YOU'VE TAKEN STOCK OF YOUR space and your needs, you'll be in a much better position to determine the cost of your project. If all your bathroom needs is a style update or better storage, you can accomplish either in a short time with a do-it-yourself skill set or a local handyman.

If you're going to replace all or most of the components of the bathroom, you're going to be looking at a significantly larger investment. A midrange bath remodel of this type can cost $5,000 to $25,000, depending on who is doing the work and where your home is located.

The cost and complexity of your project will increase significantly if you add or move plumbing; add, move, or remove walls; add to your home's electrical panel to handle new capacity needs; add a window; or create an entirely new bathroom where none existed before.

These changes usually involve permitting from your local building department, which means you'll need a licensed professional to plan and manage the process and more time to get needed approvals along the way. A project like that can easily cost $50,000 or more.

Creating a spacious new master bath can be a lengthy, costly process. This is particularly true if you're moving or adding new lighting and plumbing elements. This is the type of project where an experienced designer and contractor can help you avoid costly errors.

Updating a powder room can be a more affordable project, especially if the plumbing is staying in the same place. Updated finishes and fixtures can freshen the room and a decorative lighting fixture, such as this eye-catching chandelier, can replace a recessed can light.

more about...
BUDGET-FRIENDLY BATHROOM IDEAS

There are definite ways to save money on a bath remodel. To start, it's important to know what you want and need so you don't end up changing your mind or the project scope along the way.

KEEP WHAT YOU CAN

If you can meet your goals by keeping the walls, doors and windows, plumbing, ventilation, and electrical in place, doing so will save both time and money on the project.

DO WORK YOU'RE COMFORTABLE HANDLING ON YOUR OWN

Make sure you realistically have both the time and skill to handle the parts of the project you choose to tackle yourself. Very knowledgeable homeowners can act as their own general contractors, hiring needed tradespeople and doing the work they can themselves, but this can be as demanding as having a second full-time job.

INVEST WISELY FOR THE LONG TERM

It is tempting to buy the unbelievably affordable shower set online. It is priced that way because the knockoff doesn't use the quality components or finishes of the original, or because it's a counterfeit. The few hundred dollars you save up front can cost you thousands down the line if the valve fails and you have to destroy your remodeled shower walls to replace it.

Choose new fixtures that can also save water or energy from reputable brands and professionals. These will pay for themselves over time in durability and lower utility bills.

hiring bath professionals

● ● ● REACH OUT TO SEVERAL TO DETERMINE which one is the best fit for your project. He or she should respond in a timely manner, show up on time, answer your questions in a respectful way, and have successfully completed comparable projects, ideally in the local area. If you're only doing a modest suburban bath, someone who primarily does downtown penthouse projects may not give your job the time and attention it deserves. You also want a professional with excellent listening skills, references, and the licensing and insurance required for your project.

A smaller bathroom that just needs a fresh look can be handled by an interior designer and handyman. They can swap out a dated mirror, paint, faucets, sconces, unattractive toilet flush lever, and vanity knobs. These small details can add up to big style without a big budget.

WHICH PRO TO HIRE FOR WHICH PROJECT

ARCHITECTS

If you are adding a room to your house, an architect will help ensure that the addition works well with your existing home, pull the necessary permits, and oversee the project.

Your architect will refer or bring in a building contractor to do the actual construction, and potentially a bathroom designer to help you choose and buy the cabinetry and other elements to outfit your bath.

DESIGN-BUILD FIRMS

An alternative to an independent architect for a bath addition is a design-build firm. These incorporate both architectural designers and construction professionals. They likely also have a bath designer on staff and represent good-better-best cabinet lines for you to choose from. Their approach is to provide a turnkey project. This is a convenience, but can come at a higher cost.

BATHROOM DESIGNERS AND INTERIOR DESIGNERS

If you are remodeling an existing bathroom or converting another room to a bath within your existing walls, a bath designer—usually listed as a kitchen and bath designer—or a residential interior designer can meet your project needs. Your designer can suggest a general contractor to oversee the demolition and construction.

GENERAL CONTRACTORS

A general contractor is the construction manager on a project. GCs, as they're often called, hire, schedule, and manage the specialists (called trades in the industry) needed for the electrical, plumbing, carpentry, tiling, and other tasks that go into a bathroom addition or remodel. Contractors will often partner with designers to create the plans and choose the materials and finishes.

ABOVE Creating a new shower isn't typically a DIY project. A bath designer and contractor, working with a plumber, tile installer, and glass company for the enclosure will all be involved in creating your new space.

RIGHT While a skilled handyman can install any of the elements in this simple yet elegant bathroom, a knowledgeable bathroom designer, architect, or contractor will ensure that your project meets local codes, best practices, and any accessibility concerns you may have.

the master bath

● ● ● THE MASTER BATH IS A FAIRLY RECENT development. Previously, houses didn't have a separate bathroom for the homeowner; the entire family shared one.

As homes started to get larger, master bedrooms were often built with their own en suite bathrooms, which typically can be accessed only through the master bedroom. This created a private space with bedroom, attached bathroom, and one or two closets. Larger suites got sitting rooms, morning kitchens, and other amenities, too, but a bedroom with its own bath exclusively for the homeowner has become a standard house feature.

A master bath project should accommodate all users' needs, as well as provide new features and functionality. This room's large shower with a bench and soaking tub with a view offers fresh comforts, a spacious layout, and abundant natural light.

ABOVE Adding a master bath to create a new suite can involve sacrifices because of space constraints. A small pedestal sink and compact shower offer functionality in a tight space, while a unified color scheme and layered lighting make this small bathroom appear larger than it is.

ABOVE RIGHT One popular master bath trend is combining the tub and shower area into a shared "wet room." This often lets the tub deck serve as the shower's bench and makes good use of the space.

BELOW RIGHT This bathroom project offers a large double vanity with drawers for the homeowners, but saves space by not walling off the toilet area. This also allows light from the window to shine throughout the entire space.

more about...
ADDING A MASTER BATH TO YOUR ATTIC

One of the most popular additions to a home is a master bath or master suite. Depending on a home's zoning and lot, you may not be able to add another story or have room to expand your footprint. This drives many an attic conversion, taking advantage of untapped space and plumbing lines directly below. Attic suites also offer the privacy and quiet of being on their own level, and often provide interesting architectural details (and challenges).

THE MASTER SPA

master baths are not only growing larger, but they're also getting more luxurious. Part of what's driving this trend is the frenetic pace of modern living. The master bath has become a sanctuary for an overly stressed homeowner. It's a well-appointed chamber for starting the day and a peaceful retreat at the end of a hectic one.

The master spa will definitely include an amenity-rich shower. It may include steam or body sprays, a rain showerhead, and a massaging handheld one. It will almost certainly have a built-in shower bench and probably a niche or two for shampoo, soap, shave gel, and other necessities.

Many will be barrier-free, meaning that there's no raised threshold to step over. Most will include handsome surfaces. Sleek linear drains are a popular upgrade for spa showers, as well.

The latest addition for spa showers is digital controls. These let two users program their individual water temperature and setting (e.g., massage) preferences and start their customized shower with a single click. Extras like chromatherapy and Bluetooth® for music or news are also gaining popularity for home spa showers.

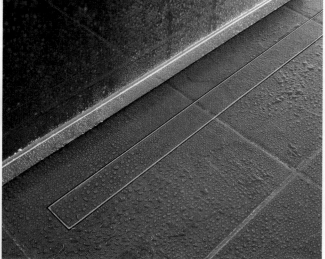

ABOVE Digital showering systems are a recent innovation. They can typically be programmed for multiple users, so that each one can get the desired temperature, flow rate, and mode with one click.

ABOVE RIGHT Linear drains, whether tiled in as shown or in a coordinating metal finish, add sleekness and drain placement options to a spa shower. These placement options can locate the drain in an area less likely to be tripped on by a mobility-challenged user.

RIGHT Handheld showerheads with massage settings offer a comfortable alternative to spa tubs. They use far less water while directing the spray easily to a sore muscle.

FACING PAGE Many spa showers today are incorporating curbless entries for style and accessibility, which works particularly well with the clean lines of this modern bathroom. These barrier-free spaces need proper planning to keep water from flowing into the room.

plan your master bath remodel

● ● ● THE SCOPE OF YOUR REMODEL WILL BE determined by your needs assessment and space. Are you borrowing from an adjacent room to expand your bathroom? Or are you staying in the existing footprint?

• space

The space you have available for a remodel includes the square feet in the existing bathroom and any you can take from adjacent rooms. Fixture clearances are set by building codes and practicality.

You can gain a little extra room by removing a wall separating a water closet from the main bathroom, or replacing it with a narrower partition made of a thinner material.

You can also create usable space by converting a standard door to a pocket door. This frees up room you would otherwise need for a door swing. A contractor can tell you whether that's feasible.

• storage

You can enhance your storage by purchasing a similar size vanity with more drawers and organizers. If there's ample countertop space, you can also add a tower for more storage.

• fixtures

If you have the space, you may want to expand the shower or separate it from the tub. Homeowners also often want to go from one to two sinks, typically requiring a larger vanity. This may involve reconfiguring the space. Other popular fixture upgrades include spa shower features, toilets with better performance, and bidet functionality.

• amenities

There is a long list of amenities available for master baths, including radiant floor heating, built-in towel warmers, window seats, remote-controlled window coverings, entertainment features, and much more.

ABOVE A partition instead of a standard wall can help you squeeze more into your small bath remodel. There are numerous material options available for this purpose. The one you choose should work with the overall style of the room. In this case, an eclectic combination of materials works in an eclectic bathroom.

LEFT A tall storage unit can add extra capacity while taking up limited floor space. This is commonly a cabinet that is ordered with the same materials, finish, and hardware as the vanity for the most cohesive look.

ABOVE Every successful bath project starts with a design plan based on your needs and space. This bathroom was carefully planned to accommodate all of the storage needs of its users while maintaining its clean modern lines.

LEFT A stylish new trough sink can definitely imbue a bathroom project with updated style, but often entails additional changes like a new countertop and faucets. These need to be factored into the planning and budgeting process.

kids' baths

●●● WHILE OFTEN CALLED "SECONDARY" BATHS and considered less of a priority than a master remodel for many homeowners, kids' baths can be fun to update and personalize.

Your reasons for redoing this bathroom might be to make it a nicer place to get ready for school or bed, or to gain storage or functionality as toddlers turn into school children, then teens.

A good option for some families is a Jack and Jill bathroom. These share a tub and toilet in a central room, but have a separate vanity area on each side with separate entrances to adjoining bedrooms.

Children's bathrooms need a tub for bathing when they're too young to shower. You'll find that a handheld showerhead can be a great convenience for washing them and the tub afterward. A rolling storage bench can be a helpful addition to a bathroom for young children. It will hold bath toys not in use and give parents a movable place to sit while bathing their kids. Shower curtains, rather than shower doors, make it easier and more comfortable to reach into all areas of the tub.

A bathroom can grow with your kids from childhood through their teens. Paint, artwork, and shower curtains are easy elements to replace as their tastes change. Built-in storage and hooks accommodate more than one user, and baskets hold everyone's gear in pretty containers.

Colorful tile and wallpaper dress up this game room bathroom used by kids and their friends. The heater and fluffy bath mat ensure that no one gets too cold while bathing after a day of fun. The bench makes it easy for a parent to help a child in the tub.

ABOVE LEFT Kids' bathrooms can be fun and stylish spaces, reflecting the child's personality and interests. These can certainly change over time, making neutrals ideal for tile, countertop, and fixtures. Add color with more easily replaced paint, textiles, and accents.

ABOVE RIGHT Even a toilet can be chosen to express style while also conserving water. The decorative detail on the skirt and lid, along with the decorative flush lever, tie into the room's personality and elevate it above a standard commode.

more about...
CHILDREN'S BATH SAFETY

Some older homes still have showers that are not temperature-limiting. If your home has never been updated, this is a definite must-change to avoid scalding a bather.

- Outlets should be GFCI (ground fault circuit interrupter) to protect against the kind of deadly shocks that can occur in wet environments.
- The bathroom floor and bottom of the tub should both be slip-resistant. A grab bar on the tub wall is also helpful for avoiding painful falls.
- Make sure that the bathroom ventilation is working properly. A non-functioning vent fan can allow mold to grow, which is unhealthy for everyone, but especially for those with respiratory or allergy issues.
- Countertop edges should be rounded so that if an active child bumps against it, it will reduce the risk of injury.

the guest bath

●●● IF YOU'RE FORTUNATE ENOUGH TO HAVE an extra bathroom for the comfort and convenience of overnight guests, you're going to want to update it with their needs in mind. Regardless of whether they're seniors or young children, safety features, good lighting, and appropriate ventilation will immediately improve the bathroom's usability. Features should include slip-resistant flooring, task lighting at the vanity for shaving and applying makeup, a quiet, properly working vent fan, and a grab bar for getting in and out of a tub.

Other conveniences like a shower seat and a handheld showerhead will enhance the space. If you're just looking to add style to the room without any renovations, fluffy towels and bath mat, an attractive shower curtain and hooks, new accessories, and a rich new paint hue can easily and affordably upgrade an existing guest bath.

You can also stock the medicine cabinet with extra toiletries your guests might have forgotten at home, and keep a hair dryer handy for guest use. These hotel touches will be appreciated.

LEFT Guest bathrooms don't need a lot of storage, unless your visitors tend to stay for extended periods. If not, a simple pedestal sink can work in the space. Lever handles make it easier for an older user to operate the faucet, and mirror-flanking sconces cast a flattering light.

FACING PAGE A chair or stool to sit on while dressing adds a touch of comfort in a guest bath. Gauzy window coverings add privacy without blocking out light. The neutral palette, elegant sconce, and gold mirror frame communicate sophistication, something a guest may expect from a hotel bath.

the powder room

● ● ● POWDER ROOMS CAN PACK A LOT OF STYLE power into a small space. All they typically include is a sink, toilet, mirror, and lighting. Also called half baths—because they lack a full bath's tub—powder rooms are mainly used by party guests and household members when spending time in the nearby kitchen and living areas.

Powder rooms don't need vanity storage due to their limited use, but they should be well lit with a good-size mirror for the benefit of users freshening up their makeup and checking their hair.

It's not uncommon to find a pedestal, wall-mounted, or console sink in a powder room. If there is no cabinetry, a cart, table, stand, or basket for storing extra toilet paper within reach is helpful.

ABOVE A piece of storage furniture in this powder room provides a place for holding extra bath tissue and guest purses. It also coordinates with the sophisticated color palette and eclectic modernity of the compact powder room.

RIGHT Console sinks are a popular choice for powder rooms, which typically need less storage than full bathrooms. They can also communicate the room's style in a single fixture, as this one does with its vintage-inspired lines and faucet.

ABOVE It's easy to splurge on finishes in powder rooms, given their compact size. The antique-inspired mirror and sconce may be too expensive to double for a master bath, making it perfect for this small space.

LEFT Pedestal sinks save room in small powder rooms, while still delivering style. The old world inspirations for the sink and toilet are shared by the beadboard wainscoting around the room and vintage-inspired faucet.

ADDING GLAMOUR TO YOUR POWDER ROOM

Powder rooms' small size and scope allow you to splurge on decorative elements that might be cost-prohibitive in a large master bath. You'll still want to design it to complement the surrounding rooms.

COLOR IT RICH

Maybe you didn't want emerald or burgundy paint in your dining room and chose a soft neutral there. Those jewel tones can work beautifully to enrich a powder room and will add dramatic contrast to a white toilet and sink. Put the neutral on the ceiling.

FIX UP YOUR FIXTURES

Change your sink and toilet for a coordinated pair in a style befitting the space. There are dozens of designer suites available to choose from. New faucets, mirror, and lighting that fit the room's new style will also enhance the room.

DRESS IT UP

Even if you're not remodeling, you can add glamour to a powder room. Upgraded accessories can improve the room's style. So can a decorative rug on the floor and art on the walls. An attractive new window covering tied to the room's new style can also improve a room's look.

work with your space

● ● ●

MOVING WALLS, DOORS AND WINDOWS, PLUMBING, ELECTRICAL, AND ventilation can add thousands of dollars and weeks or months to your project. If you have the option to leave major components where they are, that is always going to be your best option.

That doesn't mean you can't add functionality or style. Both are extremely doable and working within your existing footprint will save you stress, as well as time and money. For example, if you've just returned from a European vacation and want a bidet in your bathroom, it is more cost-effective (and space-saving) to add a bidet toilet or bidet seat to an existing toilet rather than adding the plumbing components and rearranging the room layout to accommodate a stand-alone bidet.

In most bathroom projects, it's possible to add or improve storage and lighting, conserve more water, enhance your showering experience, and update the room's style all without changing the footprint.

Enhancements like the onyx vessel sink, handsome Arts and Crafts-inspired cabinetry, stained glass window, mosaic deck, and paneled ceiling can make the most of your existing footprint. Keeping some fixtures in their current locations can create significant savings in a remodeling project.

Sometimes, however, you do need to change the layout of an existing bathroom to get the functionality you want, or you need to add an entirely new bathroom to your home. Both require extensive planning and usually professional help. You may also need building department permits, so it's best to establish your project requirements before you plan, design, and budget for your project.

ADD STORAGE TO AN EXISTING LAYOUT

TAP INTO UNUSED SPACE

There are many often overlooked areas of your bathroom that can be used for storage. A shelf with decorative baskets or bins could be installed above the door; if there's room, a cabinet could be installed above the toilet or shower; a piece of storage furniture could be added to an unused corner of the bath; and an unused side wall is the perfect place for a tall shallow or recessed cabinet.

REFURNISH AND ACCESSORIZE

Instead of a delicate vanity stool, consider a rolling storage bench. Instead of a single or double towel bar, install a row of hooks to quadruple your towel and robe capacity. Instead of bare shower or tub walls, add a hotel style towel shelf above the spray zone. If you are going to change the vanity and have extra wall space above the counter, add a storage tower there. (Outlets behind it create a great spot for storing and charging an electric toothbrush, water flosser, and shaver.)

ADD ORGANIZERS

If you have a vanity in your bathroom, enhance it with tiered drawer organizers, back of door organizers, and U shelves that fit around your plumbing for extra storage space.

BELOW An ottoman or hamper stool can add seating and storage to a bathroom. It can also be topped with a tray for added convenience when bathing.

RIGHT Sometimes, otherwise-fabulous bathrooms lack storage, but it's possible to add capacity without remodeling. In this bathroom the charming pedestal sink means that items that would normally be stored in a vanity need another location.

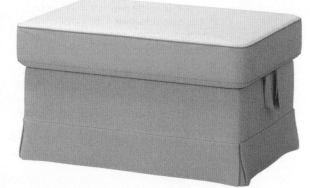

TIME FOR A REDO?

TOP A shallow recessed cabinet can be built into a wall between the studs to take advantage of otherwise wasted space. Locating it on a side wall would mean losing some of the pretty wainscot tile, but adds a tremendous amount of storage to the room and complements its style.

ABOVE A wall cabinet can add storage for bathroom staples, like extra rolls of toilet paper, and can be easily installed where it will provide needed storage capacity, in this case above the toilet.

change your footprint

● ● ● THERE ARE TIMES WHEN CHANGING YOUR footprint is the only way to get the improvements you desire. You may want to create an oversize shower with a stand-alone tub, for example. Perhaps you want to create two separate sinks or two separate vanity areas. Each brings added functionality—and added investment in time, money, and space.

Making major changes to a bathroom requires careful planning and, usually, building permits and skilled professionals. Before you take a jackhammer to your existing space, consider the clearances your changes will require. Clearances are those spaces around a fixture that allow you to use it comfortably and safely.

There are generally two sets of clearance standards. The first is driven by building codes and meets minimum requirements for modern living. The second one will accommodate accessibility, should a user of the bathroom ever need a wheelchair, walker, or other assistance.

Though everyone in your household may be perfectly fit and healthy today, following the accessibility standards will yield a more spacious, functional, and attractive space now, while supporting possible future needs. If you create an accessible bathroom, it can also enhance your home's value, as demand is greatly increasing for them.

Creating a separate shower and tub often requires footprint changes, especially when accommodating oversize and enhanced fixtures. Steam showers require space for their steam generators and spa tubs need room for their mechanicals, in addition to their own lavish proportions.

Sometimes your goals can be met with scaled-down fixtures and a creative layout. This tiny tub takes advantage of otherwise wasted floor space below the window, but still can be used for bathing a child or a stand-up rinse. The compact space is also optimized with a hotel rack that holds robes, towels, and spare items on its shelf.

clearances needed for fixtures

● ● ● ONCE YOU'VE DETERMINED YOUR NEEDS and how much of your existing footprint you'll be changing, it's time to start planning your space. There are simple tools for doing this, like graph paper and an architectural scale, but working with a layout program may be easier. You can buy a software package or use one of the many free layout tools available online.

Scaled plans, whether done by hand or electronically, will help you determine how best to accomplish your goals for an attractive and functional space. Like a jigsaw puzzle, the pieces need to fit together well for the best picture to emerge.

The National Kitchen & Bath Association has developed a set of planning guidelines that many professional designers use for creating or remodeling bathrooms. Following them will also help you comply with local building codes.

Space allowances can overlap so that the clearance in front of your master bath's new double sink vanity can double as clearance in front of the freestanding tub, for example, and the toilet can share clearance space with a pedestal sink in a small powder room. Factoring in the fixtures and their clearances will help you determine which layout type makes the most sense for the new bathroom.

DOOR CLEARANCE

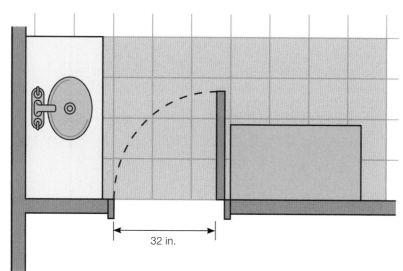

32 in.

Allow for at least a 32-in. doorway and for unobstructed clearance when the door is open at 90°.

SINK PLACEMENT

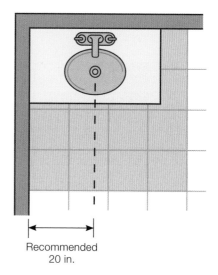

Recommended 20 in.

When positioning your sink, consider elbow room by measuring from the center of the basin to adjacent walls or obstacles. The distance should be 15 in. to 20 in. For a double sink, the distance between the centerlines of the two basins should be at least 36 in.

VANITY HEIGHT

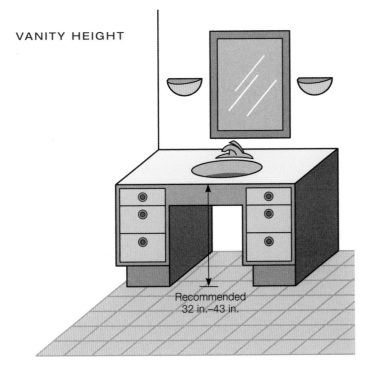

Recommended
32 in.–43 in.

Vanity height is an important issue and depends on the comfort of the user. Most users feel comfortable with a height between 34 in. and 43 in.

SHOWER SIZE

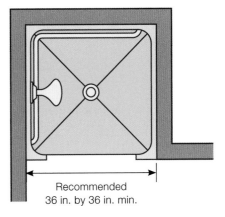

Recommended
36 in. by 36 in. min.

A shower requires a minimum of 30 in. x 30 in. For optimum comfort, consider more space.

TOILET PLACEMENT

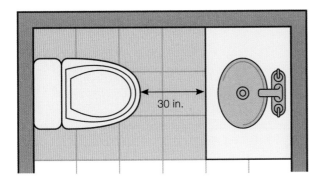

30 in.

For comfortable use of the toilet, the distance between the center of the toilet basin and any side wall or fixture should be at least 15 in. To meet universal standards, minimum clear space in front of a toilet should be 30 in. x 48 in.

CEILING HEIGHT

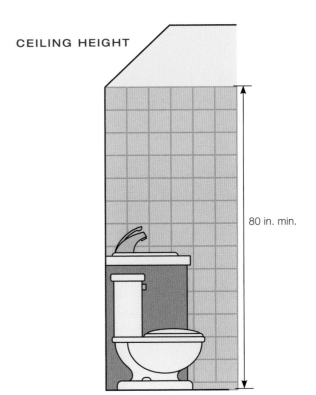

80 in. min.

The minimum ceiling height is 80 in. when the ceiling is over a fixture. Shower heights should be 80 in. as well.

layout options

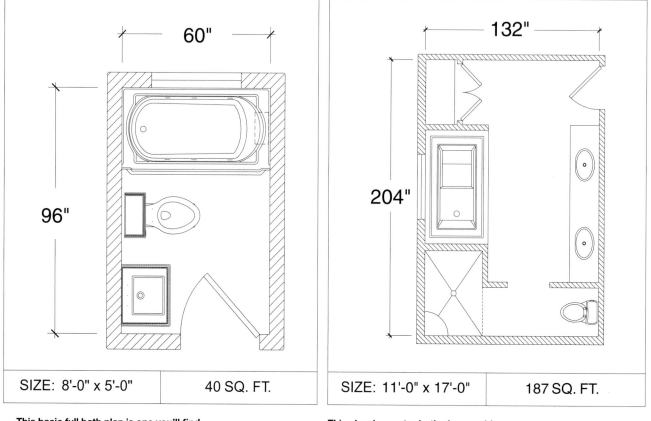

● ● ● THERE ARE SOME STANDARD LAYOUT styles that could work for your space, or you may find yourself adapting one to better fit your needs and home. Some common layouts are shown here, but don't restrict yourself to just these. You can expand or contract them as your unique space requires; just don't cheat the clearances! It is better to have a single sink vanity with enough space next to the toilet than a double vanity jammed against it. (That probably won't pass inspection either.)

BASIC FULL BATH

60"

96"

| SIZE: 8'-0" x 5'-0" | 40 SQ. FT. |

This basic full bath plan is one you'll find in millions of homes; it's often used as a kid's or guest bath.

CLASSIC MASTER BATH

132"

204"

| SIZE: 11'-0" x 17'-0" | 187 SQ. FT. |

This classic master bath plan provides space for a separate shower and tub, double vanity, and semiprivate toilet.

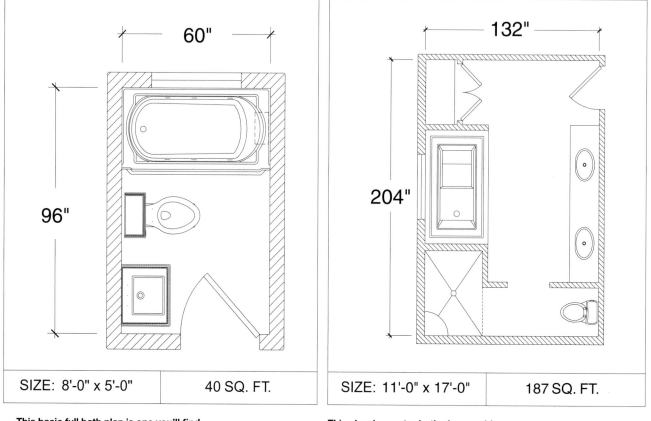

LUXURIOUS MASTER BATH

JACK AND JILL BATH

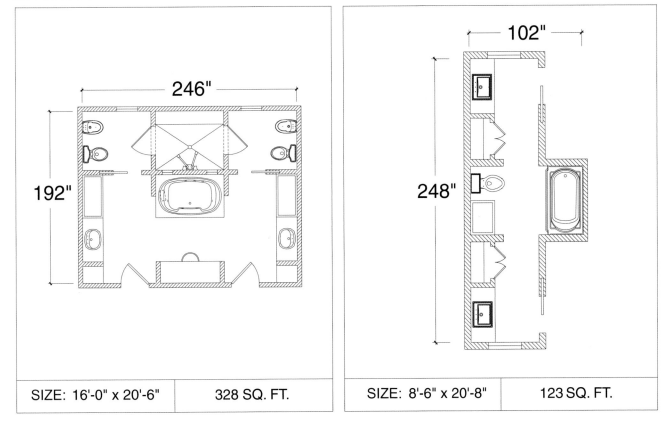

| SIZE: 16'-0" x 20'-6" | 328 SQ. FT. |

| SIZE: 8'-6" x 20'-8" | 123 SQ. FT. |

L-SHAPED MASTER BATH

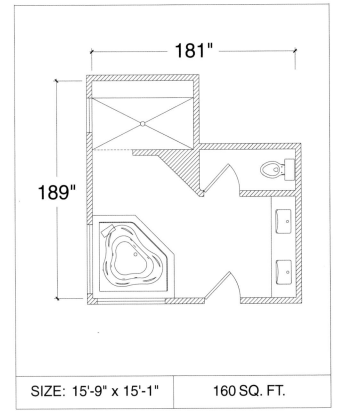

ABOVE LEFT This large, luxurious master optimizes privacy and functionality for dual users with two water closets and separate vanity areas.

ABOVE RIGHT Jack and Jill bathrooms are ideal for families with two children, as both can use their own sink area to get ready for school or bed faster.

LEFT This L-shaped layout could easily steal space from an adjacent room's closet to create a separate shower and tub, enhancing a master bath's footprint.

| SIZE: 15'-9" x 15'-1" | 160 SQ. FT. |

add a basement bathroom

●●● A HALF OR FULL BATH CAN BE ADDED TO a basement (especially as an alternative to expanding your home's size), but this approach is not without its challenges. Low ceilings and a lack of natural light are the most common problems, but basements may also be cramped, cold, and moisture-prone.

If you're creating a half bath to serve a newly finished play room, space won't be as big of an issue. A toilet and compact sink can easily meet the need. The natural chill of basement spaces won't be much of an issue either, as no one will be bathing or showering in the space. For a full or three-quarter (shower, not tub) bathroom serving a new basement bedroom, radiant flooring technologies that don't require cutting into the slab can provide comfort for bare feet and very efficiently warm the room. A good lighting plan can overcome the room's lack of natural light.

Regardless of your bathroom's size, it's going to have a toilet. But a basement bathroom's plumbing needs are different, as they may be below the local sewer lines, making gravity flush systems unworkable. (Check with your local building department for this information.)

An up-flushing toilet system is one option to address this situation. Composting toilets and sewer-ejection systems are additional options, but they are not without their limitations. Whatever option you choose, it's best to work with a licensed general contractor when dealing with the unique plumbing needs of a basement bathroom.

A well-designed, well-lit basement bathroom can be a functional and stylish addition to your home. While many basement bathrooms don't benefit from natural light, a layered lighting plan and light colors can make the space seem brighter.

A basement bathroom can present some challenges, like connecting to the home's drain lines and avoiding cold and dampness, but these can be overcome with professional plumbing help and radiant floor heat. Warm wood finishes and crisp white fixtures and tile visually enhance the room.

add an attic bathroom

●●● CONVERTING UNUSED ATTIC SPACE INTO a bedroom suite is a popular project, especially for masters. It provides privacy and often unique architectural character, especially if you're able to add dormers and windows for extra space and light. (An architect can help ensure that these additions fit with the exterior character of your house.)

There are some concerns to keep in mind with attic bath projects. First, consult with a structural engineer or licensed general contractor to make sure that the attic's support structure can handle the weight of the fixtures, users, and, potentially, a tub full of water.

Second, your attic is likely to be hotter in the summer and colder in the winter than the existing spaces in your home. It might require insulation or even an extension to your home's central heat and air conditioning system to be comfortable. It may also benefit from its own tankless water system to deliver hot water efficiently.

Last, but definitely not least, is there enough room to stand at the sink, toilet, and shower? Seven and a half feet is the minimum, and not every attic affords enough headroom. Planning where to place your fixtures will be influenced by this limitation.

RIGHT This attic bathroom maximizes the floor space below an angled wall with a storage cabinet that doesn't require full headroom. There is still room above it for some usable countertop space, smartly lit by recessed lights.

FAR RIGHT Attic bathrooms need to be carefully planned so that showers and fixtures have the headroom they require. Placing the sink and shower where you have full height access will accommodate standing use for both.

FACING PAGE It's not uncommon to have to work with tight spaces in attic bathrooms. These spaces weren't built for tubs, vanities, and other bathroom features. You'll also need to ensure that the floor is structurally sound to accommodate the weight of tub, water, and bather.

convert a room to a bath

● ● ● SOMETIMES, LOSING A SPARE BEDROOM is worth it to gain an extra bathroom. This is especially true in homes without an en suite (attached, private) master bath. A local real estate professional or appraiser can guide you on the costs versus benefits of making this change in your area. If a den conversion or stealing space from an adjacent room, rather than eliminating it, works instead, you'll be better off than reducing your home's bedroom count.

If the room you're converting backs up to a bathroom or sits above the kitchen so that you can tap into existing water, vent, and drain lines, this can offer significant savings.

Wherever you're adding a bath to your home—attic, basement, or in between—you will almost certainly need to get a permit from your local building department, so that your new bath is considered "legal." This will probably trigger a reappraisal of your property's tax value, but will be helpful if you or your heirs sell your house in the future.

Sometimes converting a room or a closet to a bathroom means you're working with a compact space. In those instances, a compact fixture like a wall-mounted corner sink can be a great asset in maximizing limited floor space. Creative wall coverings personalize the new space for its users.

An adjacent bedroom can be converted to an en suite bathroom, thus creating a master suite. It's worth talking to a real estate agent familiar with your neighborhood to determine the impact of these changes on your home's value before proceeding. If there's a half bathroom above or below it, that can reduce the cost of plumbing the new space.

hot trend
THE ECO-FRIENDLY BATHROOM

Since Earth Day was first celebrated in 1970, environmental awareness has not only grown exponentially, but it has also become enshrined in local building codes and embraced by manufacturers.

Part of what's driving this trend are drought conditions in major swaths of the country. Water conservation has become a need, not just a nicety. The EPA introduced its WaterSense® program to encourage companies and consumers to buy products that reduce use, and it is expanding rapidly. Codes have taken toilet consumption from its old 3-plus gallons per flush (GPF) to a national standard of 1.6, with 1.28 and even 1 or less becoming more widely available. Performance has always been an issue at the lower GPF levels, but manufacturers are addressing those problems with new technologies. For more information on eco-friendly fixtures, see pp. 80–82.

Water conservation has impacted showers and sinks, too, with innovations that reduce water usage while maintaining performance. New technologies that blend air and motion with water make showers feel more luxurious and vanity faucets that operate by motion sensor reduce wasted flow.

Energy use is another eco-issue. Incandescent lights, once a staple in U.S. homes, are being phased out. Fluorescent and LED lighting have replaced them, with LEDs offering greater flexibility in dimming, color rendition, and style range. (Some major manufacturers are phasing out fluorescents altogether in favor of LEDs.)

Indoor air quality is also a concern for many, with the accompanying realization that some of the cabinetry and flooring outfitting our bathrooms may be impacting our health. New laws and materials are making it easier to find products that are safer for your home and the planet.

Cabinetry using glass panels instead of wood is both eco-conscious and ideal for a full bath's moist environment. It won't warp, as poorly made composite wood can, and it adds a contemporary element to the space.

Hands-free faucets reduce water waste and the spread of germs. They are gaining popularity among families of school-age children who are most prone to leaving the water running or bringing home colds and flu bugs.

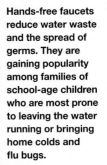

ABOVE New toilets use far less water than older models while still delivering solid flushing performance. An earlier generation toilet might use 3 gallons or more to flush; newer models are in the 1-gallon range.

LEFT Water-saving showerheads add air or motion into the spray to make it fuller and enhance the feeling of luxurious drenching. This helps meet strict new water usage codes in drought-prone regions of the country.

universal design

●●● UNIVERSAL DESIGN IS WORTH CONSIDERING for at least one full bathroom in your home—ideally on a first floor—even if there are no household members who presently need its accessibility features. Many otherwise healthy individuals have surgeries, injuries, or accidents at some point in their lives that temporarily impact their mobility.

Having a bathroom that you can still use with crutches or while confined to a wheelchair makes life immeasurably easier during a difficult time. Having a bathroom that a mobility-limited friend or relative can use while visiting your house is an added benefit.

A universally designed bathroom makes it possible for anyone at any age or mobility level to use all of its features. The doorway should be wider to allow a wheelchair to roll through. There should be ample room for that chair to roll up to the different fixtures in the room and turn space where needed.

The toilet should be higher to make transfer easier. The sink should be at a usable height for a seated user, and installed in a cabinet or countertop that allows the user to roll a wheelchair's footrest under. The shower should also be roll-in, without a curb. There should be lever handles on the shower set and sink faucets that can be operated by someone with compromised grip strength.

There should also be grab bars installed for safety, but they need not look institutional. Manufacturers are now designing them in finishes and trim styles that match their faucet and accessory sets. A universally designed bathroom can have an upscale spa look and enhance the value and "visitability" of your home.

This award-winning bathroom with its massive framed mirrors, decorative light fixtures, matte black faucets and accessories, and handsome tile and stone surfaces shows that a universal design bathroom can look more like a resort spa than a rehab hospital room.

LEFT A lowered countertop, pull-out storage, and lever-handle faucets make this vanity area highly accessible, without sacrificing modern style. Its penny round tiled backsplash, modern sconces, slab front cabinets, widespread faucets, and geometric knobs all contribute to a sleek master bath update.

RIGHT Barrier-free entry, handheld showerhead, and grab bar make this a very accessible space. To make it less institutional than a large white shower without a threshold and glass enclosure could be, the niche is covered in the same fun penny round tiles as the vanity splash and tub niche.

ABOVE The decorative grab bar, handheld showerhead, and unobstructed tub deck make bathing possible for this mobility-challenged homeowner. The penny round tiles continue from the vanity area into the tub space and the grommeted window covering coordinates with the shower curtain for a synchronized look.

aging-in-place design

●●● AGING-IN-PLACE DESIGN IS SIMILAR TO universal design, as it incorporates planning to allow ongoing use by an older resident. That resident may not have accessibility issues when the bathroom is remodeled but is planning to remain in the home for decades to come. As those decades pass, vision, mobility, grip strength, breathing, balance, and other currently strong faculties can become temporarily or permanently reduced. Rather than having to remodel the bathroom a second time, features are added to the plan to accommodate future needs. In addition to incorporating universal design features, an aging-in-place bath may also have enhanced lighting for weaker eyes, curved countertop corners to reduce the injury potential if they're struck during a fall, a shower bench and slip-resistant flooring for offsetting balance issues, a humidity-sensing fan to address memory and respiratory challenges, and a handheld showerhead with massage features to soothe arthritis aches.

The tub that visiting grandparents use may be the children's regular bathing spot. A grab bar can benefit both older and younger users in reducing painful falls.

ABOVE Coordinating grab bars in the toilet area complement the bathroom's faucets and accessories, while making the space more accessible for all users. Placing them on adjacent walls makes it easier for users to sit and stand more comfortably on their own.

LEFT A vertically installed grab bar near the entry to a shower stall reduces the chances of falling while getting in and out. This one coordinates with the shower set's lines and finish so that it blends seamlessly into the space.

find your style

● ● ●

STYLE IS THE OVERALL APPEARANCE OF A SPACE, CREATED BY ITS many components. When you walk the aisle of a bath store, you'll see rows of faucets, sinks, towel bars, tubs, and the many other elements that go into creating not only a functional space but also that space's style. The choices can be overwhelming, but they don't need to be.

Your home already has a style, as do you. Chances are there are shapes, finishes, and details that you naturally gravitate toward. These can be the building blocks of your bathroom's style. Your choices should fit comfortably with both the home's overall design and with how you live.

It is less important to know the label for the style you like or are looking at (e.g., is it traditional or transitional?) than it is to create a space that flows together well, and fits into its setting.

When shopping, ask about the maintenance requirements of the looks you love: Does that faucet need to be wiped for fingerprints every time you use it, or does that tile need to be sealed and polished on an annual basis? A designer, architect, or even showroom associate can help you pull together the elements that will create a cohesive style that works for your lifestyle, home, and neighborhood. (Because a bathroom project is a major long-term investment, it's often wise to factor resale considerations into your style planning, especially if you're unsure of how long you'll stay in the home.)

This eye-catching bathroom merges elements from modern, traditional, transitional, farmhouse, and eclectic styles. It even gets a touch of steampunk from its vanity sconces.

traditional styles

● ● ● TRADITIONAL ISN'T A SINGULAR STYLE, IT'S a collection of styles that honor the past. Traditional spans farmhouse to manor house, casual to formal, romantic to rustic. It doesn't truly matter whether the influence is English, French, or Italian; what matters is that the details work with the room and your home. To create a traditional bath, start with the largest elements, like cabinetry, fixtures, countertops, and tile, and pair them with faucets and accessories that complement their shapes and finishes.

• classical

Classical styles often incorporate heavy moldings, natural stone tile, decorative detail (like claw feet or carved valances), and faucets with elaborate shapes. A room with classical architecture does not need to be outfitted with classical furnishings as this may make it feel too formal. If your taste and the adjacent spaces are formal, however, continue the theme with classical styling. Or you can update a classical space with a few modern elements, while still preserving its overall traditional feel.

• romantic

What makes a space romantic? For a bathroom, it could be elements like crystal knobs, antique chandelier, feminine paint color, soft window treatments, floral wallpaper, glass-front cabinetry, and other details that evoke an older era or European getaway. When creating a romantic bathroom, be conscious of the tastes of other users, and avoid making a space more precious than may be practical for daily use.

• cottage

Cottage style typically fuses traditional with country and romantic, but there are also cottage styles that skew more rustic, eclectic, or even modern. The common elements are usually cozy compactness and historic design references. These references might include encaustic-look floor tiles, decorative wall paneling, or a console or pedestal sink.

Whether your cottage bathroom recalls Old England or the Old West will be determined by your taste and your home's other influences.

This romantic traditional bathroom evokes European charm with its wallpaper, upholstered chair, and window awning. The black-and-white color scheme with pops of color makes the room inviting and exciting.

TOP Gold embellishments throughout the space highlight the traditional character of this bathroom, while the sunshine pouring through the airy white drapes and the clean-lined tub give it a touch of modern freshness. Even the focal point tile tub splash wall blends traditional pattern with a modern application.

ABOVE All of the details come together to create this grand traditional bathroom. Crystal knobs, beveled mirrors, marble floors, crown molding, French doors, and decorative chandeliers all communicate history and elegance.

RIGHT Cottage style uses traditional elements like pedestal sinks, enhanced trim, and hexagon and subway tiles but does so with a casual touch. Its feeling is Old World, but without heavy formality. You see that in this bathroom's simple sink lines, wooden bench, and wall sconce.

modern styles

● ● ● JUST AS WITH TRADITIONAL DESIGN, modern styles encompass a wide range of looks and influences. Your home does not need to be modern for modern styles to work in them either. Some of San Francisco's famed Painted Lady Victorians have very modern interiors now. The simplicity of modern design's looks can complement traditional architecture. Just be consistent in the surrounding spaces to create a sense of design cohesion.

• european

European style's sleek lines, glossy finishes, and minimalism add a level of sophistication to a room without visual clutter. Floating cabinetry with lustrous paints or warm veneers, countertops with integral sinks, sleek faucets with architectural shapes, wall-mount toilets, oversize porcelain tile slabs for floors and walls, and graphic tiles that add a punch of color and pattern to an otherwise simple canvas are all hallmarks of modern European design.

• loft

Loft styles tend to add industrial chic and eclectic elements to modernism. Many homeowners who live in converted factories, firehouses, and other adapted spaces blend the quirky character of their homes—be it exposed pipes, distressed flooring, brick walls, or tall vintage windows—with minimal furnishings that let the architecture star.

Salvaged fixtures, repurposed storage, and historic tile with a modern edge—e.g., penny round tile—are all hallmarks of modern loft style.

• organic modernism

This is modernism that not only wants to look natural, but also strives to be as eco-friendly as possible. Flooring may be sustainably harvested bamboo for a powder room or locally sourced ceramic or porcelain tile for a full bath. Cork is another flooring material that can fit well into an organic modern bathroom. Some of the hallmarks of this style also include VOC-free paints in colors inspired by nature; dramatic countertops made from recycled glass or porcelain; and faucets and showerheads generous in their sleek, nature-inspired style, while being stingy with water usage.

RIGHT This bathroom embodies soft modern style. Its slab-front cabinetry is crafted from warm woods, while its cool, neutral shower wall tiles are offset with charming glass mosaics. Gentle green tones—in the accent tiles and natural stone countertop—create a soothing effect.

BELOW Modern style can take a natural turn, too. Here, elements like the rustic countertop, organically shaped vessel sinks and pendants, and tiles that evoke earth and trees give an organic feel to the space. The ambient light adds to the effect.

ABOVE This compact bathroom embodies contemporary European style. The wall-hung sink, wall-hung toilet, and sleek wall-mounted storage unit keep the smooth floor uncluttered and make the space feel larger than it is.

transitional styles

● ● ● TRANSITIONAL STYLE BLENDS TRADITIONAL and modern design. It takes its cues from classic looks, but removes all of the excess detailing for simpler, more modern lines. It's an excellent choice for a couple with conflicting tastes. Both will find elements in transitional style that they feel comfortable with, and both can bring in influences from their preferred style and have it work in their shared space.

• arts and crafts

This style is often used interchangeably with Shaker style, as both celebrate simplicity and craftsmanship, and both were a reaction to excess and imitation. Arts and Crafts honors the natural, with rich woods in clear finishes and basic shapes, and natural motifs in decorative elements (like botanical or animal relief tiles).

Shaker style, rooted in the same European and American traditions, goes further in its simplicity and lack of adornment. It has its roots in an eighteenth century religious sect and is even more austere than Arts and Crafts, though more recent interpretations favor painted wood over bare wood.

Both feature simple, square, recessed panel doors on cabinetry and furniture, whether it be quarter-sawn oak in Arts and Crafts or painted white, gray, or taupe in Shaker. A Shaker or Arts and Crafts bathroom will also feature unfussy moldings on its cabinetry and simply styled, historic-inspired light fixtures.

Arts and Crafts styling is evident in this master bathroom. The tiled mural of trees speaks to the artistic, while the Shaker-inspired cabinetry and moldings characterize the beauty of simple craftsmanship.

• steampunk

Steampunk, sometimes called Modern Industrial, is modernism paired with eclectic antique-inspired elements. It was created from creative interpretations of fantasy and science fiction literature, the Industrial Revolution, technology, and romance. It is both historic and futuristic in its approach, and can be very personalized. Black is a common color and retro clocks a common motif. Industrial shapes and artifacts are often included, or they inspire the look. Steampunk is loft style's more eccentric sibling.

RIGHT Steampunk blends historic and industrial elements in an eclectic style. Here it shows up in the subway tile, exposed copper piping and faucet, light fixture, and commercially inspired wall organizers.

RIGHT Coastal style is designed to evoke a relaxed day at the beach. Here it appears in the sand-colored floor tile, sky-blue walls, woven mirror frame and fan blades, and window shutters, so typical of homes near the water.

BELOW Modern farmhouse style tends to blend transitional, modern, and eclectic elements. The sinks and ceiling pendants are literally old school. The rustic wall paneling, pipe, and exposed stone bring to mind an outbuilding, while the wall sconces and floor read contemporary.

• coastal

Just as farmhouse style evokes the country, coastal style pays tribute to the beach. It is often rendered with traditional or transitional cabinetry, but includes ocean-inspired colors and decorative details. A coastal bath might have blue or green walls, wicker or rattan details, and an antique-inspired ceiling fan hanging from distressed driftwood planks.

• new farmhouse

Modernism meets country in the new farmhouse style. Shapes lean more toward modern design than traditional cottage looks. But country style informs the materials chosen, like reclaimed wood or stone. Repurposed sinks evoke shed, rather than manor, and a tub may be freestanding, but with a plain base rather than claw feet.

eclectic styles

● ● ● ECLECTIC BATHROOMS EMBODY MULTIPLE styles, or one primary style with added eclectic elements from another to create a customized space. This style may also be achieved by adding personalized elements like a custom carving, mural, stained glass window, or unique tile treatment. The eclectic style is all about flexibility and individuality.

This tends to work better with modern or transitionally styled rooms than it does with classically styled rooms, where the eclectic elements may clash or appear to be a mistake rather than a creative expression. The sleeker canvas of modernism or more flexible one of transitional styling better accommodates eclectic accessorizing.

The creative blend of materials, styles, and finishes makes this bath eclectic and interesting. A modern design lover will appreciate its floating shelves, towel ladder, and freestanding tub. A traditionalist will admire the tiled wall, decorative chandelier, and console sink. Both styles work together well in this creative space.

The playful purple tiles and sleek fixtures create an eclectic space that doesn't take itself too seriously. The unadorned floating vanity and wall-hung toilet enhance the room's feeling of openness, making it feel cooler, lighter, and more refreshing than the dark floors and walls would suggest.

more about...
BLENDING STYLES TO PERSONALIZE YOUR BATH

Sometimes you blend styles to express the tastes of two people with contrasting visions. Sometimes you blend to tie a new space to an adjacent room you're not remodeling. Sometimes you blend to create something uniquely you. Whatever your reason, there are terrific ways to make it work well in your home.

Unify finishes. One way to combine two different styles is to choose elements with the same finish. New contemporary polished chrome accessories can update a space with traditional polished chrome faucets.

Make it personal. Use decorative elements to express multiple users' personalities. In a shared children's bath, for example, decorative accent tiles can reflect each of the occupants' favorite animals, or a wall niche can display a shared collection of family vacation memorabilia.

Update the elements. New wall paint, shower curtain, artwork, bath mat, and towels can add traditional, eclectic, or modern style to a bathroom easily and affordably.

THE ELEMENTS
THAT CUSTOMIZE

your bathroom should be a reflection of who you are, not just a generic space. While creating a cohesive look, there is room to personalize it with elements that will make you smile. This could be a decorative tile inspired by a vacation you took to Mexico or Morocco. If the overall style works with the look you're creating for the room and budget allows, you could use it generously to cover an entire floor or tub or shower surround. If it's a splurge, or not something you want to see on an entire surface, an accent treatment for a display niche could work instead.

Sinks, lighting fixtures, and even cabinet hardware can all be used to personalize a space. The shape can evoke a hobby, like a floral knob for an avid gardener or starfish for a beach lover. Even a detail as small as a drain can add a touch of your personal style. Look for ways to express your personality, interests, and memories subtly in the details of your bathroom.

Decorative tile is one of the easiest ways to build your personality into a bathroom project. By creating a custom focal point element like a backsplash or floor medallion, you can add a favorite place reference—perhaps Morocco or Spain—that speaks to your family's history or heritage. The pattern and color will tell their story in ceramic, porcelain, or natural stone.

Shower drains have evolved from basic rounds to include stylish finishes, shapes, and details. You're no longer limited to a small, hole-filled disk to express your design personality. The wave pattern on this drain complements the stone floor, evoking a rocky coastline.

ABOVE Cabinet hardware can express your hobbies and interests, like gardening and nature. This silver branch-shape cabinet pull evokes the forest and feels particularly at home on the rustic wood cabinet doors.

LEFT A mosaic sink inspired by historic architecture can evoke a breathtaking vacation memory. Its shimmering tiles add instant glamour and personalized beauty to the space.

how to choose a style for your bathroom

●●● YOUR HOME'S STYLE (OR STYLES) WILL help determine the style for your new bathroom. Powder rooms and pool baths typically serve kitchen, great room, patio, and dining room areas—i.e., the "public" spaces in your house—and are thus part of the "entertaining flow." You can opt for the same flooring, wall tile, and faucet finishes as the other rooms. You don't have to carry everything through, but your guests shouldn't feel as though they've wandered into a different home entirely when they visit these bathrooms.

Your master bathroom's style should take its cues from the master bedroom to create a cohesive suite. Elements like lighting, cabinetry, window coverings, and paint can easily extend across both spaces. The same is true for half baths next to a home office or playroom.

Hall baths often serve the household's children or resident grandparents. While they should fit the overall look of the house, it's easy and affordable to incorporate the personalities and preferences of their users with paint, towels, shower curtains, and artwork. The major design elements—like fixtures, flooring, and cabinetry—should flow with the home's general style.

RIGHT The light palette and details of both rooms make this master suite feel cohesive. The door hardware style and finish in both bedroom and bathroom coordinate with the faucets and accessories. The white tile floor of the bedroom is echoed in the smaller and more slip resistant tile of the bathroom.

FAR RIGHT Powder rooms may take an independent style route from their surrounding areas, while still incorporating some of their design elements. Flooring is often a shared surface, continuing from a hall or great room. The selected countertop coordinates beautifully.

The Arts and Crafts cabinetry in the bathroom takes its inspiration from the bedroom set.
The paint and overall color schemes are also shared between the two connected spaces.

UPDATE USING YOUR EXISTING STYLE

CHANGE YOUR SINK FAUCETS

Sink faucets are far easier to replace than tub or shower faucets, and this small, affordable change can easily improve the style of the room. You'll want to stay in the same finish to complement what you have in the other fixtures and same configuration if you're keeping your countertops and sink.

UPDATE YOUR HARDWARE AND LIGHTS

You can also add affordable style with new cabinet knobs and pulls, a flush lever for your toilet, and towel and robe hooks. Keep them in the same finish as your faucets for some consistency, but look for those that will freshen up the room in a style that inspires you. With cabinet pulls, opt for new ones with the same hole spread so that you don't have to create new holes in your cabinet doors and drawer fronts or cover old ones. Even lighting fixtures are fairly easy to change if they're staying in the same spot. Tie those, too, into your faucet and hardware choices.

VANITY COUNTERTOP AND SINK SET

If your vanity is a standard width and depth, you may find a new countertop and sink set in stock at your local home center or bath showroom. Measure your vanity's width and depth, and factor in whether it's a double or single. If you're keeping your sink faucets, you'll need to consider their configuration, as well, so that the drilling in your new set will accommodate them. This can deliver a significant style punch to your bathroom without a significant investment of time or money.

RIGHT A few easy replacements can add updated style to this bathroom.

A new quartz countertop with undermount sinks will add style and easier maintenance to your vanity area.

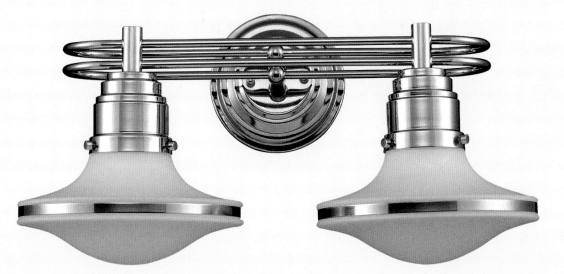

A new LED bath bar adds energy efficiency and midcentury modern style to the bathroom. Both are timely updates that improve this space.

A new widespread faucet will fit into the holes in the existing countertop, or into a new predrilled quartz top if it's being replaced. It will also use less water, while updating the room's style.

New cabinet knobs are the easiest and fastest change you can make to a room. To keep a consistent look, make sure your new knobs coordinate with your faucets.

master bath style considerations

● ● ● YOUR MASTER BATH SHOULD TAKE ITS style cues from your master bedroom. If you're updating the bedroom at the same time, design them with a common style. It's also worth considering those styles you have loved the longest, rather than something you just discovered, for such an important and lasting project.

Your master bath is the space you will start and end each day with for decades to come, and it should feel welcoming, comforting, and refreshing to you. A style you have loved for years is the likeliest to fit this description.

ABOVE The Arts and Crafts bed and built-in storage in the master bedroom coordinate with the bathroom cabinetry for a cohesive master suite.

RIGHT While the overall look is unified, the bathroom cabinetry has different hardware that complements, rather than exactly matches, the bedroom built-ins.

CREATING A PULLED-TOGETHER MASTER SUITE

harmonize the style of your master bath with your master bedroom, even if there is a door between them. If they're sharing the same private suite, they should flow together visually.

Take furniture cues. Your master bed and bedroom suite should inspire the shapes and finishes of your bathroom cabinetry. They don't have to come from the same source, but they should share a similar look, as each is a major visual component in its space.

Share lighting styles. An attractive light fixture in the master bedroom can lend its style inspiration to the fixtures in the bathroom.

Continue the flooring. Even carpet and wood lovers can carry the material's color into the tile for the bathroom flooring. This color can be carried over as an accent color in the tile or as its dominant shade, which will also make the spaces look larger. New porcelain tiles in realistic wood looks can go from the bedroom right into the bathroom, creating a greater sense of space and coordination. (It is not, however, a good idea to try to match the wood exactly with wood-look tile in the bathroom.)

Style coordination between bedroom and bathroom is especially crucial in an open master suite. Here, the ceiling beams and white walls unify the space, as do the white cabinetry and tub, which echo the white bedding.

powder room style considerations

● ● ● YOUR POWDER ROOM SHOULD TAKE ITS style choices from the rooms it serves. A modern kitchen and dining room will work best with a modern powder room, for example, with related finishes and shapes.

At the same time, powder rooms offer the opportunity to pack a dramatic style punch in a small space. Rather than try to create an entirely different look, maximize the complementary style with an element that might be too bold or costly to use on a larger scale. For example, a brilliant paint color that coordinates with the surrounding rooms or a scaled down but dramatic ceiling light fixture.

ABOVE This modern powder room would coordinate beautifully with a modern great room and kitchen. The stainless-steel countertop and chair rail can echo stainless-steel kitchen appliances and the warm wood paneling may be carried onto a great room wall or cabinetry.

RIGHT This eclectic powder room uses a stunning tile along one focal-point wall. To create a cohesive look, this wall tile could be used as a kitchen backsplash or on a fireplace surround. The bronze details of this room would find a perfect complement in kitchen faucets and lighting fixtures.

FACING PAGE This spacious powder room's flooring and architectural woodwork would be right at home in an adjacent living space. It comfortably blends coastal and farmhouse styles with its color scheme, artwork, paneling, and charming fixtures in a way that could easily be extended throughout the home.

fixtures and faucets

●●●

THINK BACK TO THE BATHROOM OF YOUR CHILDHOOD. IT PROBABLY had a basic tub and shower combination, a toilet, and shared sink. Until fairly recently, bathrooms were compact spaces to accomplish simple tasks.

That basic bathroom was a huge advancement from the shared washtub in the kitchen and outdoor plumbing of previous generations, but today's homeowner has so many more choices. Bathrooms have evolved far beyond the basic into personal spas for master suites, style showcases for powder rooms, aging-friendly spaces for parents and in-laws, even fun spaces with flair for the younger members of the household.

Chances are, of all the bathrooms in your home, you're going to make the largest investment in your master bathroom. Rather than a simple tub-shower combination, your master is more likely to have a separate soaking or whirlpool tub. Your toilet is more likely to have its own private room within a room and, potentially, bidet features. It will almost certainly use far less water than the toilet you grew up with; building codes are getting far stricter on this point. Your toilet may even have increasingly popular hands-free flushing or self-cleaning features.

Bathrooms have moved beyond basic and utilitarian in recent years, especially master bathrooms. They have grown in size and status. In place of tub-shower combinations, you will often see stand-alone "statement" tubs.

Your needs, space, and budget should shape the choices you make in the bathrooms you remodel, but so should real estate trends in your neighborhood in case you decide to sell your home.

sink types

● ● ● BATHROOM SINKS COME IN SEVERAL different types, with practicality, style, and budget often determining which ones you choose.

• drop-in/top-mount/ self-rimming sinks

These are typically the most affordable sinks with rims that sit on top of the counter and predrilling for faucets.

• undermount sinks

These are designed to install under the edge of a vanity top for a more upscale look and easier maintenance. They are often paired with stone tops and are professionally installed. A variation on the undermount sink is the apron front, which has an exposed side for decorative purposes. It may also add increased size to the fixture with its extended facade.

• console, pedestal, and wall-mounted sinks

What these have in common is that they don't require a cabinet and countertop to rest on. Consoles with two or four legs are often selected for their aesthetic value, whereas wall-mounts are typically chosen for their compact size. Pedestals may be selected for both style and space reasons.

• vessel and wading pool sinks

These style-forward sinks sit on top of a countertop. Vessels are often made of unique materials and tend to be highly decorative. Their bases can be difficult to clean around because of their shape, and they require wall-mount or special vessel faucets to accommodate their height. The self-rimming wading pool sink is really a shorter vessel that may be more comfortable for petite users.

• integral sinks

Integral sinks are made of the same material as the countertop and typically have imperceptible seams where the edge meets the sink. They are often found in solid surface tops for budget bath projects, and in glass, porcelain, composites, engineered stone, and concrete for upscale spaces.

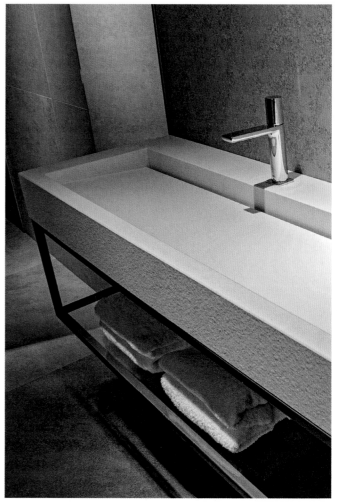

Integral sinks are often selected for their clean, contemporary lines, which also make integrals easy to clean. It's not uncommon to see them with minimal or hidden drains to enhance their sleekness, and in trough lengths for double vanities.

BELOW The popular wading pool sinks are essentially shallower vessel sinks (or taller top-mounted models). They offer the style profile of the once-dominant vessels, while not necessarily requiring their specialized faucets and generally being easier to clean around.

ABOVE Apron front sinks have long been staples in traditional and transitional kitchens. In recent years, they've started appearing in master bathrooms, too. Their larger dimensions can make some tasks easier—like washing your hair at the sink or hand-washing delicates.

LEFT Like pedestal sinks, console sinks are frequently chosen for their slim profile, relative to vanities, but lack their closed storage. What they seldom lack is personality! This one contributes to the charm of the colorful pop art–inspired bathroom.

fixtures and faucets   75

sink materials •••

•ceramic

Ceramic, especially vitreous china, is one of the oldest and most common bathroom sink materials. It is easily cleaned, but also easily chipped or cracked. Some new pricier versions have very durable, ultrathin sides.

•cast iron and cast steel

Cast iron is also a very old material and one of the most durable. It includes a metal core and high gloss enameled surface. Today's leadless cast iron won't necessarily perform quite like Grandma's did, though, and may rust at drain and faucet connection points.

Cast iron's heavy weight is another drawback, and has given rise to the cast steel sink. The core metal is lighter, more flexible stainless steel. These can be installed without bracing but are likelier to crack than cast iron.

Ceramic sinks are among the most widely available in the bathroom category. The latest models bring their low-maintenance and durability to a new sleekness with ultrathin sides. The thinness doesn't compromise strength, given new production techniques, but does add tremendous style.

•solid surface, resins, and composites

The popularity of solid surface countertops has led to the integral solid surface sink with its low-maintenance seamless appearance. Despite their soft feel, these sinks are fairly durable and repairable if damaged.

Resins and other man-made composite materials are also molded into integral sinks. These range from affordable cultured marble sets to fashion-forward troughs. Their blend of engineered materials creates a countertop and fixture with smooth and easy-clean surfaces.

•the exotics

Sinks can also be made from glass, natural stone, copper, pewter, bamboo, and even wood. Glass is among the most common, with the lowest maintenance, and is more durable than its reputation would imply. Natural stone, copper, wood, and concrete, on the other hand, require regular maintenance.

Glass sinks can be modern or traditional, decorative or simple. This versatile material creates a beautiful, unexpectedly durable, and easy-care fixture that makes a definite statement in a bathroom project.

ABOVE
Manufacturers have been producing composite sinks, made of different types of materials blended together for easy maintenance and durability, for a long time. Once relegated to the budget category, composites have gotten more sophisticated and stylish in recent years. This sink's soft gray meshes beautifully with the room's neutral palette.

ABOVE Metal sinks are more commonly found in kitchens, but make a strong style statement in a bath. They come in mirrored, matte, or hammered finishes, depending on the desired look. Metal sinks also come in different shapes and installation types for design flexibility.

LEFT Exotic materials, like the onyx shown here, other precious stones, wood, or bamboo, are selected for their dramatic appeal. These exotics often require special care that homeowners should consider before choosing them.

sink faucets

● ● ● LIKE SINKS THEMSELVES, THE FAUCETS that serve them come in multiple formats, materials, and price points. If you're just replacing a faucet, not remodeling the sink area, look for a model that will fit the same holes. You have more options today than in the past. Manufacturers have learned that not everyone wants their faucet spreads to be predetermined at a standard 4 or 8 inches. Flexible water and connecting lines and interchangeable parts are also included in some packages to allow for customization at the time of installation.

faucet types

The most common are 4-inch centers, 8-inch centers (also called widespread), single hole, and wall-mount. Wall-mounted faucets are harder to replace. In addition to differing installation types, there are also differences in handle types, from aging-in-place-friendly lever handles to knobs and cross-hatches.

There are also new hands-free faucets that can be turned on with an arm tap or wave motion, but you will need to manually adjust their temperature and flow rate.

faucet materials

Faucets may be clad in metal, resin, or combination finishes, but their construction is commonly solid brass or a brass substitute with other non-corrosive materials. Flow regulators can be rubber O-rings inside a brass cartridge, ceramic disks, or metal or plastic balls. The best quality faucets will generally be solid brass construction with ceramic disks.

Finishes vary widely. Brushed nickel, oil-rubbed bronze, and polished chrome are among the most widely available and affordable, but other metals, spot-resistant treatments, and even composite faucet finishes are gaining popularity.

TOP LEFT Single-hole faucets are popular options, especially for wading pool sinks and compact installations. There are taller versions available for vessel sinks, as well.

LEFT Widespread faucets, also called 8-inch faucets because of the traditional distance between their handles, are an upscale alternative to centerset models. Some new widespreads can be installed with the handles closer than their name implies, which can be helpful in tighter spaces.

Wall-mount faucets are a terrific option when you're tight on countertop space, or when you're using a vessel sink and don't want to use a vessel faucet. Wall mounts come in traditional or contemporary styles, but can be more challenging to install or replace.

water usage

In 2006, the Environmental Protection Agency created the WaterSense program to help conserve water, a vital resource. There is a tremendous selection of WaterSense-labeled sink faucets to choose from today, each certified to be 20% more efficient without sacrificing performance. In many parts of the country, water conservation is a requirement of completing your permitted remodel, and these faucets can help you achieve it.

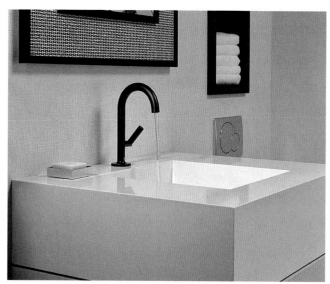

ABOVE Centerset faucets, also called 4-inch faucets because of the distance between their handles, are among the most common models on the market. That makes replacing them easy, as there are so many styles and finishes to choose from, often in very affordable price points.

LEFT Once found only in public restrooms, hands-free faucets are now becoming mainstream in residential baths. They offer the benefit of reduced water use, as they'll only stream while hands are in sensor range. These faucets also reduce the spread of germs, an ideal feature in shared bathrooms.

m o r e   a b o u t . . .
UPDATING YOUR VANITY FAUCETS FOR A NEW LOOK

Vanity faucets make a big impression for their small size, and the sink or countertop-mounted types are easy to replace if you stay in the same configuration or find a customizable model.

UPGRADE COMPATIBLY

If the other styles and finishes in the room are traditional and polished chrome, you'll create a better look if you upgrade in traditionally styled polished chrome. You can still upgrade your faucet's appearance and performance, but be mindful of style cohesion.

UPGRADE COMFORT

Perhaps your grip strength isn't what it was when you first moved in, or you dislike the feel of the knob currently installed. Replacing your faucet gives you the chance to select a handle that feels more comfortable to your hand. In most cases, a lever is easier to operate than a knob.

UPGRADE QUALITY

Perhaps the builder installed a basic plastic ball handle faucet that cost a pittance at the local faucet depot. You now have the opportunity to upgrade the quality of your faucet, while delivering better style in the process.

Widespread faucets
with lever handles
deliver traditional
style and ease of use.

toilets, urinals, and bidets

● ● ● TOILETS ARE ONE OF THE MOST common fixtures in any home. Your bathroom may not have a tub or shower, but it will have a toilet, also known as a commode.

• toilet types

The most common types are one-piece and two-piece, but wall-hung toilets are becoming increasingly popular for their height flexibility, ease of cleaning, and space savings. Round bowl toilets also deliver space savings over oval bowls, but are less comfortable for the average adult.

Comfort height toilets are an alternative to wall-mount if both accessibility and affordability are concerns. They are generally 2 to 3 inches taller than a standard toilet, making it easier and more comfortable for many adults to use, and simpler to install than a wall-mount.

• water conservation

One of the challenges for the plumbing industry is to make toilets that deliver performance while using less water. Before conservation standards, a toilet would use up to 6 gallons to flush. Code today mandates a 1.6 GPF, with WaterSense-rated toilets at 1.28 GPF and an increasing selection using 1 gallon or less.

Expectations are that the national code will adjust to the WaterSense level, so it's worth considering for your project. Dual flush toilets that let you choose between higher and lower water volumes based on need also conserve.

• urinals

Some homeowners choose urinals for the convenience of male users. Adding a urinal instead of a second toilet can significantly reduce your bathroom's water usage.

• bidets

These plumbed basins with their directed water jets are traditional in many cultures for personal hygiene, but take up precious floor space. An excellent alternative is a bidet seat, or a toilet with bidet features. Both enhance hygiene, but do not require the plumbing components or clearances for a second fixture.

TOP Some homeowners are opting to bring urinals into their residential baths. Once a fixture exclusively found in commercial restrooms, urinals offer convenience and water savings at home, too.

ABOVE Two-piece toilets, with their separate tank and bowl, are extremely common in American homes. They come in all price ranges and can be simple and unadorned or more decorative for upscale projects. The transitional detail on the lid and base adds style to the fixture and the room.

ABOVE Bidets are essential hygiene fixtures in many European and Asian bathrooms. Travelers and those moving here from those cultures have popularized them in the U.S., too. In recent years, bidet functionality has been added to toilets, rather than adding a separate fixture.

FAR LEFT Wall-hung toilets are gaining in popularity, especially in universal design and aging-in-place projects. They can be hung at a height personalized for an individual user, and their in-wall tank also makes them ideal for compact spaces.

LEFT One-piece toilets combine bowl and tank in a single unit. They are most often modern in their design, as their seamless design lends itself to a contemporary project. Water closets or toilet rooms are often selected for larger masters to give privacy to the user.

THE SMARTER TOILET

toilets are offering some tremendous new features that go far beyond their original purpose and capability. Which one you opt for will be determined by your habits, budget, and where you live.

A self-cleaning toilet can be an asset in any home, as it reduces the time spent on a thankless chore. Different technologies, including ultraviolet light under the lid and the design of the bowl, make their interiors as low-maintenance as possible.

Many homeowners may also appreciate the benefit of a hands-free flushing model, as it reduces germs spread between users. There are touchless flush kits that will modify many existing toilets, but a new hands-free toilet will include the benefits of water conservation that your existing toilet may not.

A toilet with bidet functionality adds hygienic and comfort features, like intimate washing and drying, but their higher price tags are not appropriate for every project. This would be a worthwhile splurge for a master bath in a higher-end home, but not necessarily a feature you'd add to a budget remodel.

At the highest end of the luxury spectrum is the connected toilet that offers not only bidet functionality and a heated, self-raising/lowering seat but also a foot warmer and music through your electronic device. There's an increasing niche for technology-infused premium toilets in the luxury market.

ABOVE Self-cleaning toilets make a dreaded chore quicker, easier, and potentially obsolete. Self-cleaning technologies vary between manufacturers but can include proprietary bowl materials that clean themselves with a flush and ultraviolet light in the lid.

LEFT Higher-end bidet toilets can also incorporate connectivity and personalized features. This allows the user to stream music or podcast through a speaker, and summon the hygiene, drying, lighting, and entertainment features they prefer with their preset selections.

ABOVE Bidets require more space than is often available in a bathroom remodel. A toilet with a bidet seat offers the same benefits, without the cost of buying or plumbing a separate fixture.

RIGHT Hands-free bathroom technology at home started with faucets and has expanded to toilets, which typically flush with a hand wave over a sensor. Hands-free flushing toilets are growing in popularity for their hygienic and germ reduction benefits.

tubs

● ● ● FINDING A TUB THAT FITS YOUR NEEDS and budget will take some time and effort, but both are well worth the investment. Size, material, installation needs, and price will all influence your choice. You can narrow things down with research, but be sure to physically test the tubs you're considering before buying one. You'll want one that fits your body, as well as your project.

Start your exploration with a plan. Will the tub be built into an existing space, taking advantage of water lines and drain already present? If so, what are the available length and width? On which side is the drain?

If it's going to stand freely in a new area of the room, is there clearance space around it to get in and out safely? Where will the plumbing components go? Some new tubs even offer Bluetooth streaming and remote controls, but require additional connections and a tech-savvy professional to install them.

If you're planning on a larger or deeper tub, you'll need to make sure your floor structures—especially for upstairs bathrooms—can handle the additional water weight, or plan on reinforcing them.

How will you keep the water warm while you're bathing? If you're considering a whirlpool tub, also known as a spa tub, this is especially important as the jets can cool the water. It also requires accessible space for the motor and an electrical connection.

While it may be tempting to contemplate a long soak in a palatial tub, water and energy conservation requirements in your area might mean skipping this luxury. Don't buy a bigger tub than you will likely use on a regular basis.

One of the most popular tub configurations is deck-mounted. There are two options. Drop-in, as seen here, has the tub lip sit on top of the deck. It's a more affordable installation than undermounting a tub, but less uncluttered-looking.

ABOVE Bathtubs in master suites have evolved from basic tub-shower combinations to stand-alone focal points. Where to locate them becomes an important consideration, factoring in size, shape, views, and privacy.

LEFT Apron front tub-shower combinations are still a mainstay in American homes. They offer the option of stand-up showering or bathing in a single compact space, making them especially popular in children's bathrooms.

jetted tubs

● ● ● WHIRLPOOL OR SPA TUBS CAN GREATLY enhance your bathing experience and add value to your bathroom. However, they do require additional planning and space for the components that run them.

After determining your tub's size and position, you'll need to choose what types of jets you want: water or air. Air jets are easier to maintain than bacteria-prone water jets, and often have a smaller, quieter motor, but they give a softer, less-focused sensation. When trying a tub at a showroom, wear a bathing suit to experience the differences between the two for yourself.

Another option for a jetted tub is chromatherapy—the addition of colored LED lights for relaxation or invigoration. While you may be skeptical about the health benefits of this relatively new discipline, you might just enjoy the experience of a colorful glow in your tub while bathing, adjusted to your mood or taste.

LEFT Chromatherapy adds color and light to the spa tub experience. Users can choose the hue they find relaxing or stimulating, depending on their mood and preference. For added effect, sometimes a ceiling-mounted spout is chosen to create an outdoor-inspired mood.

ABOVE Some homeowners, especially those who have experienced them overseas, prefer a deeper tub like those found in Japan. These tubs are available for use in the U.S., but thought must be given to the agility of the users for getting in and out safely.

Spa tubs come with air or water jets. Air jets offer a less robust experience, but are easier to maintain. Before selecting a type, it's best to try both in a showroom.

tub configurations

●●● WHETHER JETTED OR NOT, TUBS COME in a range of configurations that fit different needs and spaces. One of the most common is the apron front tub with a finished facade that installs between three walls. These are typically designed for tub-shower combinations in smaller or secondary bathrooms.

Another type of built-in tub is the walk-in model. Designed to enable users with mobility issues to enjoy a bath, these tubs have a few drawbacks. One is that the user must sit in the tub while it is filling up and draining, both of which can be uncomfortable. Another is the cost of a walk-in tub, which is significantly more than a standard model. Last but not least, there are very limited style options that may not fit the look of your room, especially a contemporary one.

Drop-in tubs that fit into a deck and surround built to enclose them are widely used in master bathrooms. The tub's rim sits on the deck. A variation on this is the undermount tub that installs in the same setting, but is secured to the underside of the deck for a more upscale look. These are generally more expensive to purchase and install than drop-in models.

Freestanding tubs are increasingly popular in master bath projects. They come in a wide variety of shapes, sizes, and materials and are usually chosen for their style. Typically deep, they can be hard for some users to climb in and out of, so consider a user's agility and balance before choosing this type of tub.

LEFT Walk-in tubs make it possible for those with mobility issues to get in and out with greater ease. Their style and functionality have improved in recent years, with the addition of jets and handheld faucets, but a user still needs to sit in the tub while it fills and empties.

ABOVE Many tubs are dropped into built-in decks and surrounds. The wood or tile surrounding them gives the bathing area its style and personality. Drop-in tubs come in numerous sizes and shapes, with oval and rectangle the most popular.

ABOVE Freestanding tubs are becoming increasingly popular as master bathroom focal points. When selecting one, it's important to decide early in the design process what type of tub filler will be used and where it will be located. Floor-mounted models are a premium option.

LEFT A second type of tub used with decks and surrounds is the undermount model. In this type of installation, which is costlier than drop in, the lip of the tub is secured to the underside of the deck, which is often stone or quartz. A popular option is to extend the tub deck into an adjoining shower to serve as its bench.

tub materials

•••

cast iron and cast steel

Like sinks, tubs may be cast iron or cast steel. Iron will keep your water hot the longest, but these tubs are so heavy that they often require two installers and floor reinforcement. (Some plumbers and contractors are not working with cast iron now due to safety and insurance issues.) The steel version is an easier-to-install, durable alternative.

fiberglass, acrylic, solid surface, and composites

Fiberglass is among the most affordable tub materials, but it scratches the easiest and won't last as long as more durable alternatives. Acrylic and other solid surface materials offer a good, midrange option as their color goes all the way through the body of the tub and scratches can be buffed out. They also come in a wide range of sizes and shapes, often sleek and contemporary.

exotics

There are a few exotic tubs on the market like copper, stone, concrete, and even wood, but be sure to consider their resale appeal and maintenance requirements before buying one for your home.

ABOVE Copper is a stunning material for a bathtub that will create a dramatic focal point. It is a material that needs special care to maintain its original finish, though, so consider whether this is something you're willing to do, or whether there's a treatment that can be applied to preserve it more easily.

RIGHT Wooden tubs are not that common, but you will occasionally come across this option. Like stone and copper, wooden tubs require special care, but they can definitely create a nostalgic accent in a traditional or eclectic bathroom.

ABOVE Many tubs today are made from acrylic, fiberglass, solid surface, or composites, ranging from affordable to upscale. These all offer easy care and different tub configurations far beyond the basic tub-shower alcove installation.

LEFT Another exotic tub material is natural stone, prized for its beauty and elegance. Whether marble, granite, onyx, or soapstone, natural stone tubs need to be sealed for their protection. They are also exceptionally heavy, so special care and costs are involved in their installation.

tub faucets

●●● YOUR TUB'S CONFIGURATION WILL determine what faucets you'll need. Freestanding tubs often require freestanding tub fillers, though wall-mounts can work in some spaces. Tub-shower combinations almost always use a combined tub-shower wall-mounted set with a diverter that switches the flow from showerhead to tub filler. Deck-mounted tubs occasionally use a combination wall set, but much more often use deck-mounted faucet sets. These increasingly include a handheld unit to allow for standing or rinse-off use.

Handheld faucets are becoming increasingly popular for tub-shower combinations, too, especially with added features like massage settings. These handheld models are ideal for those with accessibility issues for seated showering, and for cleaning the tub and surround after use. There are also ceiling-mounted faucets that are finding favor among some homeowners and designers, especially over focal point tubs.

Changing tub and tub-shower faucets is a much more complex replacement than sink faucets. You need to know the make and model of the existing set to find a new one that's compatible with the valves behind the tile, unless you're planning on changing the valves, too. There are a few new models on the market that will work with existing valves, but verify with your plumbing contractor that they'll definitely be compatible with yours to avoid installation issues.

ABOVE While freestanding tub fillers are often selected, wall-mounted spouts and controls are a viable alternative in some settings. They can add style at a more moderate cost, and may simplify plumbing installation.

LEFT Deck-mounted faucets, also sometimes called Roman faucets, are the most common choice for stand-alone tubs in surrounds. Handheld spray add-ons are a popular feature, as they make it easier to rinse off after a bath.

FACING PAGE Floor-mounted tub fillers are a relatively new option, made popular with the growing number of freestanding tubs in master bath designs. Not only will you be choosing a compatible style, you'll also be deciding on the optimal location that's reachable from both inside and outside the tub.

tub surrounds and enclosures

●●● FROM AFFORDABLE FIBERGLASS AND composite remodeler kits with tub and walls to exotic mosaics, your bathtub may be surrounded by a wide range of materials and styles. Natural stone will deliver unparalleled beauty, but also increased cost and upkeep. Stone-look porcelain tiles are becoming an increasingly popular substitute for natural stone, with a lower price point and easier installation. Thin porcelain slabs and very similar sintered compact surfaces (with slight differences in formulation and processing) are the latest tile options and offer a grout-free alternative for even lower maintenance. Similar to porcelain, ceramic tiles have long been a popular option for tub surrounds and continue to be an affordable, widely available, and versatile choice for a variety of bathroom styles.

Tub-shower combinations require enclosures to keep the water inside, as well as waterproof surrounds. The options are glass doors or shower rod, curtain, hooks, and liner. Glass doors are the more upscale but expensive option, especially frameless styles.

For children's bathrooms, a shower rod, curtain, and hooks can be a practical alternative. The shower curtain can also add a fun style element your child can help choose. Many homeowners are installing tension rods that don't leave holes in the wall and can be removed later if desired.

Because of their design, freestanding tubs don't get standard three- or four-sided surrounds. A decorative tile treatment behind the tub can enhance its focal point presence and protect the wall against water damage.

ABOVE LEFT Shower rods with hooks and curtains are an affordable alternative to doors. Curved models add spaciousness and hotel style to the tub without remodeling, especially when choosing tension mounts.

ABOVE RIGHT Decorative tile is a popular way to personalize a tub surround. It is one of the most versatile, easy-care, and durable materials on the market. Options range from affordable ceramic to natural stone, depending on taste and budget.

Solid surface and fiberglass tub and surround sets with bypass doors are popular with builders and remodelers for their easy installation and affordability. Homeowners like their easy-care and built-in shelving options.

tub safety

●●● TRADITIONALLY, TUBS HAVE BEEN A PRIME location for accidents at home, but they don't have to be. Incorporating safety features in your tub can help you and your loved ones avoid injury.

Manufacturers are starting to offer grab bars in the same styles and finishes as their faucet and accessory sets, allowing you to integrate them into your bathroom without it looking institutional.

A common bath injury is scalding from overly hot water. There are several types of valves available to prevent this in your tub, including pressure sensitive, thermostatic, and combination valves. There are also new showerheads, both fixed and handheld, that show the water temperature before getting in, should changing the valve not be an option.

Deck-mounted tubs can be challenging for users with balance or mobility issues. Designing a wider deck so that the bather can sit and swivel easily into and out of the tub will make it safer for these users. Grab bars also help.

While it is becoming increasingly popular to install a beautiful light fixture over a tub, this may not be allowed in your space for safety reasons. Many local codes restrict the placement of any electrical elements such as fixtures, outlets, or switches within 5 feet of a tub in any direction to avoid accidental electrocution.

One other safety factor to consider is ventilation. A properly functioning vent fan can help avoid an unhealthy mold situation in your bathroom. Sensor units will turn on and off automatically as needed.

Grab bars are now available in styles and finishes that coordinate with faucets and accessories to create a more designer look. Many manufacturers now include them in their product suites, giving you more choices than ever to be safe and stylish at the same time.

ABOVE Falls are not the only risks that come with bathing. Scalding is another potential hazard. New valves that limit temperature are one development that has saved users from burns. A more recent technology displays the water temperature.

LEFT A bathroom this elegant will look for ways to hide its ventilation behind architectural features, as even the sleekest, quietest models break up the ceiling line. A sensor unit will keep it out of earshot while still doing its job to keep the air healthy.

UPDATE YOUR TUB WITHOUT REPLACING IT

ADD SHOWER DOORS

If you're upgrading your bathroom for adult users, new shower doors can make a big style impact. There are frameless models for modern style or obscure glass for easier maintenance and to conceal a less-than-attractive surround. If you're replacing an existing door, confirm the mounting system, method, and hardware before removing it, as old holes can be unsightly if not covered by the new glass and hardware. Holes can be professionally repaired in acrylic or fiberglass surrounds, but you might need to replace damaged tiles for the best results.

ADD SAFETY

There are stylish grab bars that don't require a tearout to reinforce them. Choose one that matches your style and finish to add a safety element to your bathroom, then have it professionally installed.

ADD ACCESSORIES

New accessories on the market give you the option to include attractive shelving to your tub area, adding style, storage, and convenience.

TIME FOR A REDO?

ABOVE Even the most basic and dated bathtub can be enhanced with new features that add style, storage, and even safety.

ABOVE RIGHT When the existing soap and shampoo holders are inadequate, they can be supplemented with sleek new storage accessories. Not only can this add convenience and capacity, an attractive accessory can add style to a tub, as well.

RIGHT When the tub is so basic and funds aren't available yet to replace the fixture or its faucets, a decorative door can hide an unattractive interior. It can later be used on an upgraded model, or in another one of the home's bathrooms.

FACING PAGE A designer-style grab bar can make getting in and out of the tub safer for adult or child. Choose a finish that complements the faucets for the best result.

the shower space

• • •

MOTHER NATURE DESIGNED THE FIRST SHOWERS KNOWN TO HUMANS: waterfalls. They were usually very cold. The ancient Egyptians moved showering indoors, but their systems were still cold and inconvenient; you basically used a jug to pour water over your head and body. If you were well-to-do, your servants did this for you.

It was the Greeks and Romans, many years later, who came up with the type of communal showers that athletes and spa goers use today. They loved bathing as we do, and created magnificent spaces to celebrate personal hygiene. Many homeowners today seek to do the same, and the master suite's shower has evolved into a spacious, luxurious temple of clean.

While some are still simply-equipped with a standard showerhead, many now feature multiple showerheads, built-in benches, barrier-free entries, and even steam. Whether they're styled for traditional, transitional, or contemporary bathrooms, showers all share the same hygiene and comfort goals.

When choosing from the many shower enhancements available today, consider which ones best fit your space, budget, local conservation codes, and daily needs. For instance, a carwash-style set of body jets may sound appealing for relieving frequent muscle aches, but might a handheld showerhead with a massage setting meet the same need?

Modern spa showers have largely replaced tub-shower combinations in master suites. Features like rain showerheads, handheld showerheads, and open enclosures have become popular design features inspired by resort travel.

Adding or remodeling a shower space is a major, long-term investment that will impact your physical well-being, your home's value, and your utility bills.

shower configurations

●●● THE MOST COMMON SHOWER configuration—and one you probably have somewhere in your home—is the tub-shower combination. This meets the needs of most users in the most basic way possible. You can take a bath or a shower in the same compact space. It is so common to the American home that manufacturers have come up with "remodeler sets" including affordable tubs and shower walls to fit into fairly standard 30-inch by 60-inch spaces.

The popularity of the master suite has led to separate tub and shower spaces. That, in turn, has led to showers of different sizes and shapes. Some of these showers have more than one showerhead to accommodate two users at once or different showering styles. Many have benches and an increasing number have steam.

Many homeowners have found that the tub rarely or never gets used and have started looking at shower-only master baths. Others, who still want both, have combined them into one "wet room," where a freestanding tub fits inside an oversize shower enclosure. Another popular configuration is side by side, with the tub deck extending into the enclosed shower to become its bench.

On the more modest end, there are remodeler set stand-alone showers for in-law suites, utility rooms, and compact pool baths. These have a surround, shower floor, drain, simple controls and valve, shower arm, and showerhead. Handheld models work well for in-law suites, especially if there's also a built-in shower seat and grab bar. Handheld showerheads and remodeler sets also work well for bathing larger dogs indoors.

The nested shower takes advantage of the neighboring tub deck to add into its bench. This configuration is an excellent use of space and resources, and creates visual continuity in the room.

ABOVE One recent shower configuration is the wet room. This layout has become popular in master bathrooms and puts the tub and shower into the same enclosure. In many installations, including this one, the enclosure is frameless glass.

ABOVE Stand-alone showers are an excellent option for compact bathrooms. Many homeowners are choosing not to include tubs—even in larger spaces—as they rarely use them, and are opting for enhanced features like dual showerheads instead.

LEFT Some homeowners are opting to forego enclosures entirely and create an open shower. The effect is sleek and modern, but planning must be careful to design against moisture and spray damaging nearby walls and floors.

THE ECO-PERFORMANCE SHOWER

One of the primary challenges of spacious, multifeature showers is making them eco-friendly. Local building codes across the country, driven by persistent droughts, are mandating increasingly stingy water and energy use. So while homeowners have come to expect ever-improving performance, manufacturers are being driven to create shower systems that deliver ever-improving efficiencies.

They have come up with technologies that blend air, motion, or a combination of both into the water stream to create a waterfall-like or carwash-style experience while using far less actual water. This allows homeowners to enjoy rainheads and body jets in the same space, though not necessarily at the same time any longer. The Environmental Protection Agency's WaterSense program can help you identify the most water-saving showerheads on its Website and on packaging labels.

Digital showering systems make it possible to preset the shower's temperature and flow style to each user's preferences at the push of a button, thus saving water and not having to adjust the controls every time.

There are also recycled tiles that create a handsome floor and surround for a shower, while avoiding the environmental damage that natural stone quarries can create. Although these won't impact your utility bills, they can make your project more sustainable overall.

RIGHT Body sprays are popular shower features, made eco-friendly with new conservation technologies. Most will now blend air and/or motion into the spray for a fuller feeling with less water.

ABOVE Another way to be eco-conscious in your shower, without sacrificing aesthetics, is to opt for sustainable materials. Wall and floor tiles made from recycled fixtures keep those out of landfills. Many have self-cleaning properties, as well, which can reduce water and chemical use to maintain them.

LEFT Digital showering systems save water by letting each user program his or her favorite temperature and spray mode, so less shower time or water is required to reach the desired levels each time.

CENTER Rain showerheads, like body sprays, are also popular features, but have been water hogs in the past. The same technologies that are introducing air and motion into body sprays for conservation and performance are doing the same for rainheads.

shower access and enclosures

● ● ● SHOWER ACCESS HAS BECOME AN AREA of focus as more homeowners move away from standard tub-shower combinations. How you enter and exit your shower has almost as many options as how you shower within the space. Even the tub-shower combo usually offers a choice of rod, hooks, and curtain or shower doors. In some cases, a glass partition wall that covers half or two-thirds of the shower area substitutes for standard doors and track. Stand-alone showers are often covered by a glass swing or bifold door and often have a very low threshold, making it easy for most users to get in and out.

The most elaborate spa-inspired showers frequently have a barrier-free entry. Some have linear drains at the entrance so that water does not flow onto the surrounding floor. Others are large enough so that the shower stream—or streams—do not escape into the room. These larger showers may also have partial walls or enclosures that don't extend all the way up to the ceiling to allow light in. Those with steam, however, will be fully enclosed to keep the steam in the shower space.

LEFT With the move away from tub-shower combinations, new enclosure options become possible. This zero-threshold wet room uses a glass partition wall to maximize space and light penetration. Glass tinting provides privacy for those using the space.

FACING PAGE With careful planning, a shower can be open to the room, eliminating an enclosure. This will often include waterproofing the floor and walls beyond the shower space and sloping the shower floor away from the opening.

TOP Shower drains can now serve a decorative role as well as a functional one. They come in different sizes, shapes, finishes, and patterns to enhance the design of the space in a way the original round disc with holes never could.

ABOVE Sometimes you don't want to see the drain at all. New linear tile-in drains capture water around their metal edges, with surfaces that blend into the surrounding shower floor. They may also reduce hair clogs and a trip hazard over a more open drain type.

m o r e   a b o u t . . .
SHOWER DRAINS

Shower drains used to be pretty basic: A small round metal plate with holes to allow water to leave the shower was standard for decades. Newer options include linear drains that are either decorative metal or filled in with tile that matches the floor. These have dramatically enhanced the appearance of the shower space. Some remodeler set flooring bases now even come with more decorative drain options.

Linear drains have also increased drain placement possibilities when a shower is being completely redone.

Often they're placed at the entry to a new barrier-free shower. Another popular spot is at the base of an angled bench, so that the drain doesn't have to be stepped on at all.

The newest drains sit at the bottom of a shower wall, rather than in the floor. Be conscious of the fact that clear communication between you, your plumbing contractor, and building inspector are essential to the successful completion of your shower project when considering new-to-market innovations.

shower controls

●●● BEFORE THE SPRAY FROM YOUR showerhead reaches you, a sophisticated set of plumbing controls brings in water at the temperature and rate you prefer. The controls also keep you and your loved ones from being scalded. Many homes come equipped with a pressure-balanced valve that controls temperature and flow with one handle. A thermostatic valve lets you control flow and temperature separately and can handle handheld showers, rainheads, and body sprays individually. (Some local codes require them to prohibit using multiple head types simultaneously.) The newest type is digital, offering convenience and water savings.

Where you place the controls is important, too. The recommended location lets you turn the water on and adjust it, if necessary, without having to get wet. This typically means a side wall that you can easily reach through an open shower door.

If there are two separate controls, one should be reachable that way. National Kitchen & Bath Association design guidelines set the control height between 38 inches and 48 inches above the floor. It's important to have the needs of all users, including any in a wheelchair, in mind when planning.

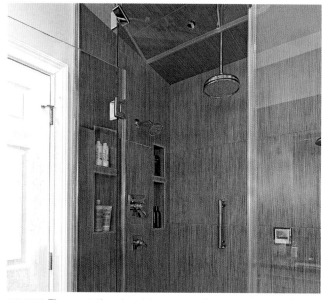

ABOVE Thermostatic valves let you control temperature and volume separately, adding more flexibility and control for the user. Many homeowners prefer them. The steam system has its own digital control, as well.

RIGHT The fixed showerhead, handheld showerhead, and body sprays can all have their own controls, but recent building codes in drought-stricken regions have mandated built-in restrictions against operating more than one set at one time. While combined use creates the luxurious drenching many users enjoy, its water requirements brought about the new stricter codes.

One set of controls is positioned near the entrance to the shower so the user does not need to enter or get wet to adjust the flow and temperature. This is a planning recommendation for safety against scalding.

showerheads

●●●THERE ARE SO MANY OPTIONS TO CHOOSE from now, both in type and style. The basic head on a shower arm is still available, but has been both enhanced and eclipsed by newer options. Many standard showerheads have gotten bigger to deliver a more rainshowerlike experience. These rainheads come in both wall- or ceiling-mount configurations. Other showerheads have built-in handheld heads for a two-in-one option. Handheld showerheads are a great option for accessibility, and are often installed either with, or in place of, standard showerheads.

Body jets, essentially mini targeted showerheads, have gotten sleeker and adjustable for users of different heights. There are also special feature showerheads that offer chromatherapy—i.e., light in different colors—to affect mood, and heads that stream your tunes or podcasts via Bluetooth technology.

What they all share is the need to deliver an effective showering experience while saving water. Manufacturers are doing this in new ways, all while delivering lower flow rates. WaterSense shower systems, which require a flow rate of 2.0 gallons per minute (GPM) or less, (compared to standard 2.5 GPM), will likely become the national standard in the near future.

LEFT The same chromatherapy features of adjustable color lights for tubs are available in showerheads. This can invigorate a user for the day's first shower or provide mellow relaxation during the last.

BELOW One of the newest features for showerheads is connectivity. Several manufacturers are now building removable speakers into showerheads or shower bars that stream a digital device's Bluetooth for music or information.

Rain showerheads remain popular for spa-inspired showers. The largest spaces can give dual users showering together their own rainhead, but local building codes will impact whether they can be used at the same time.

shower surrounds

● ● ● THE MATERIALS USED IN YOUR SHOWER surround determine not just how attractive and costly your shower will be, but also how high or low-maintenance. Shower walls of natural stone—including marble—are some of the most beautiful, but require the most care. Stone and tile grout, found in millions of shower surrounds, can also be time-consuming to keep clean and over time may need harsh chemicals or professional attention to restore it to its original color.

Ceramic and porcelain tile are versatile and popular shower surround materials. They offer endless size, shape, color, and style options that allow you to create a completely custom shower. They also range in price from extremely affordable to high end, especially when it comes to the more stylish and dramatic decorative inserts.

One of the newest trends is the oversize porcelain slab and very similar sintered compact surface (differences are slight and more marketing than technical). These offer the low-maintenance ease and versatility of tile with minimal grout. Each slab can be as large as a shower wall itself, or two might come together for a larger space.

Fiberglass, acrylic, and composite blends are all options for full wall panels and can be installed above a tub or in a stand-alone shower. Most tend to be affordable and low-maintenance, but may lack the more customized look of higher-end surfaces. Many now offer molded shelving or niches for soap, shampoo, and other necessities.

Newer solid surface options are coming on the market in more contemporary and upscale looks, and with sleek, modular accessory options. These surrounds provide the easy to install and clean options many homeowners seek, while offering style beyond typical remodeler sets.

Whatever type of shower surround you select, it's important to factor safety into it. Before installing your shower walls, it's helpful to provide bracing behind them for grab bars. Even if you don't add them now, the bracing will make installing them in the future much easier.

Not all shower surrounds are custom. Many projects take advantage of remodeler sets that come with floors, walls, and drains to make installation easy and affordable. They can still look attractive with a nice shower curtain or door.

LEFT Custom shower walls are often created from tile combinations. Here, coastal blue and gray mosaics create a dramatic focal point and combine with white and gray field tiles for an elegant installation.

BELOW Solid surface is another option for noncustom shower surrounds. Solid surface surrounds often come in modular sets with accessories for shower storage and have greatly improved their aesthetics in recent years.

ABOVE Shower surrounds can offer safety along with visual appeal. The elegant tile in this setting provides a handsome backdrop for the space, while the grab bar does double-duty as a slide bar for the traditionally styled shower set. It should be braced behind the attractive walls before installation.

more about...
SHOWER NICHES

Shower niches are built into many prefabricated surrounds, but must be planned in advance for custom showers. Many master bath projects have two niches so that each user can have ample space for his or her shampoo, soap, and other shower supplies. Niche placement is key, as you don't want bars of soap or razors to be in direct shower spray and, at the same time, toiletries need to be within easy reach. One should be accessible while sitting on a shower bench. The other can be next to it or on an opposite interior wall. When possible, place niches out of view from the shower door, so that toiletries are contained, but not seen. Considerations like grab bar bracing and plumbing line placement also need to be factored into the niche location, and the services of a professional can be very valuable in this decision-making process.

ABOVE Oversize porcelain tile slabs can create durable, low-maintenance shower walls. New production technologies are creating natural stone and wood looks on thin sheets that are easy to install and, without expansive grout lines, easy to live with.

RIGHT Custom niches put shower items where they're readily accessible for users. It's not uncommon today to find multiple niches in a shower to accommodate two users and even decorative display.

LEFT This shower combines materials from the bathroom surrounding it for total style cohesion. The white and blue floor continues straight into the wet room from the main room and the shower column features the same stunning blue stone as the vanity tops and tub deck.

ABOVE Even simple field tile—those larger unadorned pieces that make up the bulk of most installations—can create a luxurious surround when strategically designed. Here, the color combinations and contrasts create a surround with contemporary elegance.

m o r e   a b o u t . . .
SHOWER FLOOR MATERIALS

S hower floors are typically made of the same materials as shower walls, but they must be slip-resistant. Often, this means a coordinating tile in a smaller size with more grout to reduce the chance of falling. Premade shower floors, called bases, are typically designed for remodeler sets with matching walls. These are manufactured with built-in slip resistance and drains. When choosing a premade shower base, it's crucial to factor in the shower space's size and existing drain location so that your purchase lines up properly.

shower benches and seating

●●● SHOWER BENCHES IN RESIDENTIAL bathrooms are a relatively new phenomenon, and a welcome one. In years past, seats were added to showers only for those who couldn't stand for long, or at all, and they were added without regard to appearance. The popularity of shower benches in upscale hotels likely brought them into the home design sphere, and users of all abilities have found them convenient and appealing. They allow users to shave their legs more easily, sit when they're tired, and rest larger items that don't fit into niches.

There are two essential built-in seating types. One is constructed as a fixed-position bench; it is typically made of the same or complementary material as the surround and floor. These may be built into a corner for a smaller shower or the full length of a wall for a larger one. Some slant out at the top so that a linear drain can nestle underneath. Most extend all the way to the shower floor, but a few extend from the wall at seat height like a large floating shelf.

The second style of shower seat is hinged onto one wall, where it rests when not in use, and moves into seating position when needed. Water-resistant materials like teak and composites are popular for these seats. They are generally more compact than built-in benches and can be a good solution for a smaller shower stall. Hinged seats require strong bracing for safety and support.

Floating benches that don't extend to the shower floor are sometimes chosen for modern spaces because of the streamlined visual effect they create. Like hinged seats, they must be heavily braced from behind the shower wall.

BELOW Built-in shower benches have become fairly standard for master suite showers. They are typically made from the same materials and finishes as the surrounding floor or walls but can add decorative details like the contrasting seat shown here to create a focal point.

ABOVE A hinged seat that folds out of the way when not being used is an option when a built-in shower bench is not being planned. It must be braced from behind the shower wall to support a heavy user. These seats are often made out of teak or other water-friendly woods, along with sleek metal frames and hardware for attractive styling and durability.

IMPROVE YOUR SHOWER
WITHOUT REMODELING

HIDE AND EXPAND A CRAMPED, DATED SPACE

If your shower is small and ugly, but you're not in a position to remodel it, you can still improve it. Replacing a door with a curved shower rod and curtain will increase the usable space within. It can also hide the unattractive stall and threshold, giving your bathroom an easy, affordable face-lift. Just be sure to have a skilled professional cover any holes left behind by frame screws.

REPLACE YOUR SHOWER SET AND SHOWERHEAD

If you know the make and model of your existing shower set, you'll be able to determine whether there's a new trim kit available to work with your existing valve. This is a fairly simple and affordable replacement. If you don't know them, or there isn't a compatible trim kit, you can still upgrade with a new showerhead. This can be a water-conscious rainshower model or a multifunction handheld version.

ADD STORAGE

You can increase your bathroom's storage capacity with a shower arm mounted caddy in a matching finish for toiletries. This is especially helpful if your shower lacks a shelf or niche. Also consider adding a hotel-style towel rack on the wall opposite the shower arm above the spray zone. If the ceiling is extra high, you can actually install a cabinet or cabinets in the empty space above the shower to hold surplus items, but you will want to moisture-proof the bottom.

TIME FOR A REDO?

Many homes still have their original shower stalls installed by the builder. These were often selected for easy installation and affordability, rather than for aesthetic appeal. It is possible to work around these basics to give the shower area a more updated look.

A curved shower rod in a coordinating finish can add some hotel style to the space. Installed above the shower stall with a longer custom shower curtain, it can completely hide the dated builder set from the room.

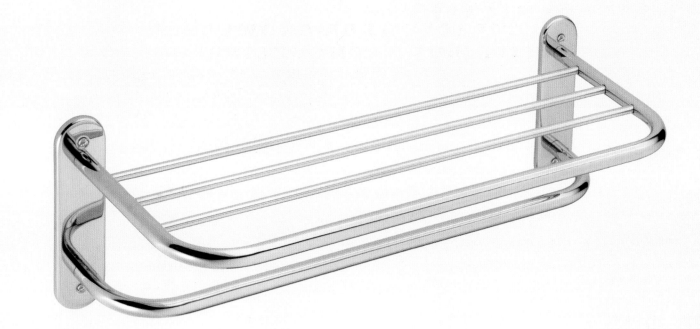

ABOVE A hotel shelf installed in the shower above the spray zone can add to the space's updated hotel style, while also adding some storage capacity to the bathroom.

LEFT There are some new "flex set" shower systems that can work with an existing valve. Selecting one with the help of a plumber can improve your shower performance, style, and water conservation. Choose finishes and lines that will coordinate with other elements in the room.

steam showers

●●● STEAM SHOWERS ARE BECOMING MORE common as the population becomes more health-conscious. They're great for relaxing after a stressful day, but also beneficial for easing allergies, asthma, and arthritis; improving circulation; and hydrating skin. That's why you'll find them at so many spas and fitness centers. Now they're showing up in master suites at home, too.

In most cases, steam showers are designed for larger spaces with a bench for two to enjoy together, but a large dual shower space isn't required. What is needed is a steam generator located close by, a steam head (like a showerhead, but for steam) to send the steam into the shower space, and a full-height enclosure to keep the steam completely within.

There are some luxury upgrades available for steam showers. These include digital controls for user personalization, in-shower audio via Bluetooth technology, chromatherapy, and aromatherapy to engage all your senses. There are even remote control options to start your steam shower from bed.

A qualified and experienced plumbing professional should be used to install a steam shower in your home; this is not a do-it-yourself project.

BELOW Full-height enclosures are essential for steam showers to keep the steam from escaping into the room, but will often have a transom window above the door. This can serve several purposes, including closing up the space when the ceiling is too high for just a door, stabilizing the glass surround, and, if operable, helping the steam escape after the shower.

ABOVE Steam showers have gained popularity for master suites in recent years. Many users get health benefits from them, beyond the relaxation opportunity. They are said to improve circulation and complexion and relieve muscle soreness often associated with strenuous exercise.

This spacious steam shower has a rare feature in its window. If incorporating a window in your project, research the availability of antifogging glass with tinting options for privacy.

outdoor showers

●●● MASTER SUITES IN WARM-WEATHER locations sometimes include an outdoor shower next to their bathroom, adding a refreshing natural element to the bathing experience. These showers are typically accessible only from the master suite for privacy, and may have high walls for the same reason. They may also have an open-structure ceiling like a trellis or a roof extension. The objective is to add openness and nature to the bathroom while still protecting the privacy of the users.

Outdoor shower sets can be chosen to coordinate with the interior shower set or to add a contrasting note of drama. These need to be outdoor-rated, though, as rainwater can damage interior fixtures. The shower flooring also needs to be outdoor-rated, due to the exposure to the elements.

ABOVE Outdoor showers can serve a master bathroom exclusively as a luxury feature, or be shared by those using a nearby pool or spa if the home lacks a dedicated pool bath. How much enclosure it gets will usually be determined by privacy requirements and how it will be used.

RIGHT Some master suites take advantage of private gardens to create outdoor showers. This gives the homeowners an Eden-like experience of enjoying a luxurious soak under sun or stars. The fixtures and flooring will need to be outdoor-friendly to avoid rusting and slip hazards.

An outdoor shower can be a simple separate space, rather than a formal extension of a master shower. It might be used by pool guests after a swim or by family after a visit to a nearby beach, with functionality as its chief objective.

125

storage

• • •

THERE NEVER SEEMS TO BE ENOUGH SPACE FOR EVERYTHING YOU want to keep in the bathroom, especially a shared one. Each occupant has his or her own grooming tools, soaps, shampoos, styling products, vitamins, and medicines. When you decide to add or remodel a bathroom, it's best to take stock of what really needs to be stored there and what can move elsewhere in your home. If, for example, you purchase bulk toilet and facial tissue, pain relievers, and other cost-saving items, it's best to keep just what you'll need for one month in your bathroom. This will leave room for hair dryers, curling irons, electric toothbrushes and shavers, water flossers, and other essentials that you use daily.

The right bathroom vanity can accommodate much of your storage needs. Some of the newer cabinets on the market have built-in plugs for keeping electrical devices charged and ready to use. There are also clever storage accessories that hold essentials. Some are designed to wrap around the plumbing, install on the backs of doors, or install behind false panels to make use of otherwise wasted space.

Bath storage can extend beyond vanities, as well. There are wall cabinets, tall cabinets, and floating shelves that can hold baskets or bins. These will all require installation, but can greatly increase your storage capacity.

Bathroom cabinetry can make a strong style statement in a bathroom. It can also add tremendous storage capacity for the everyday essentials used in this space. Floating vanities that don't extend to the floor can make a large block of cabinets feel visually lighter.

There are also freestanding furniture pieces like etagere shelving units, carts, and storage ottomans that increase capacity without requiring installation. You just need to have the floor space to accommodate them.

construction

●●● MOST BATHROOM CABINETS TODAY ARE made from composite wood products, including plywood, though there are a few made from solid wood, glass panels, and other materials. Medicine cabinets may have plastic or metal boxes with mirrored doors.

Standard bathroom cabinets are framed or frameless. The latter gives better access to the interior and is becoming increasingly common. Many bath cabinets have soft-close doors and drawers to prevent slamming. Full-extension drawer glides are also a popular, widely available feature that let you see and access your items more easily. Drawers are most commonly constructed of wood with either dovetailed or stapled corners. Dovetailed joinery generally lasts longer. Some drawer boxes—especially in upscale contemporary cabinets—are made of metal.

Cabinets are generally divided into three groups: stock, semicustom, and fully custom. Stock cabinets come in the most popular sizes and are available for fast delivery or immediate pickup. In general, they cannot be modified and cost the least.

Some stock cabinets are meant to be assembled at home. If you're having them professionally installed, their assembly will add to the labor cost, eliminating part of your savings. If they're being assembled by a nonprofessional, the integrity of the cabinets' construction could be compromised by a lower skill level.

Semicustom cabinets allow for some modifications by a manufacturer, typically depth, interior accessories, upgraded finishes, and decorative details like toekick valances. They may take up to two months to receive and will cost more than stock.

Fully-custom cabinets may be made in a factory or a local cabinet shop. Every detail from size to number of drawers to finish and decoration is made to order from either source. Manufacturing times and costs will vary greatly, but custom generally costs more and takes longer than stock or semicustom.

Stock vanities can deliver style and quality but generally don't allow for modifications of any kind. Some are available to be taken home from the store the same day, rather than waiting several weeks for delivery. Those that require assembly add an extra step to your remodel and should be done extremely well to guarantee their performance over time.

ABOVE Inset drawers and doors create a high-end look that is typically available only on custom cabinetry. Paint matching, individualized heights and widths, and creating completely unique offerings from architectural drawings and specifications are also possible with custom cabinetry.

LEFT A vanity or linen tower can be made from a repurposed piece of furniture. Adapting furniture to new uses adds sustainability to your bathroom project. It also adds personalization, especially if the piece has sentimental value.

vanities

●●● THE MOST BASIC VANITY HAS A DOOR section to contain the plumbing and is topped with a countertop and sink. (Some home centers sell sets that combine all three.) Many users want drawers to hold their essentials, and wider vanities will include at least one. Having two or three stacked drawers next to the door area is a common configuration for a smaller bath.

More elaborate vanities may have two separate door sections for double sinks and a three-drawer bank between them. Sizes can range from 24 inches wide for a very compact single model to 78 inches or wider for a double.

It's more common, though, to combine separate cabinets that are easier to get into a bathroom than to use one cabinet to create a larger double vanity area. This modular approach costs more but is easier to maneuver into place and provides more flexibility for drawer count and placement.

ABOVE A vanity can be designed from multiple cabinets to create a furniture look that exceeds what most single cabinets can achieve on their own. The bump out, columns, and decorative toekick deliver old-world charm to the expansive area.

LEFT Vanities can be small and simple, especially for powder rooms where less storage is needed. They still make it possible to keep some basic items close at hand, but hidden from view.

FACING PAGE A double vanity for two users is often achieved with modular cabinet boxes, rather than a one-piece larger vanity. This allows for more design flexibility for each user. It also makes it easier to deliver, especially with stairs and corners.

cabinetry hardware

● ● ● ANY CABINETS WITH DOORS AND DRAWERS are going to have hinges and glides. Soft-close hinges and drawer glides that were once available only on semicustom or custom cabinets are now increasingly available on more affordable stock vanities. So are adjustable hinges that make a door easier to align at installation and over time by the homeowner. Vanity drawers don't typically need to hold the same weight as a kitchen drawer full of silverware, so heavy-duty glides are not required. You are still going to want smooth motion and full extension for maximum convenience.

In addition to this functional hardware, your cabinetry might have decorative hardware. These can be knobs, pulls, or both to open doors and drawers. Pulls are typically easier for someone with wet or weaker hands to use, and are considered more aging-in-place friendly. Decorative hardware is like jewelry for your bathroom and should be chosen to complement the other design elements in the room, like your faucets and towel bars.

Contemporary cabinets might have integral pulls that blend with the door and drawer fronts. They might have no decorative hardware at all, but use hidden push latches or electronically driven openers. These are harder on the finish, though, and may create more wear and tear on the cabinet fronts in the long run. They will also create more fingerprints on gloss finishes.

Cabinet hardware is the final word on the style you've defined for the bathroom. It can communicate your preference for traditional, transitional, eclectic, or contemporary in a single piece.

Many modern bathrooms are doing away with hardware altogether in favor of integral pulls. Some will have metal edging, while others just blend into the drawers for a minimalist look. They offer the added benefit of not catching on your clothing as you lean against the vanity.

ABOVE Cabinet hardware, such as drawer handles, can coordinate with other elements in the room, like faucets, towel bars, and robe hooks. Both can share shapes or finishes to create a pulled-together look.

LEFT Cabinet hardware is your bathroom's jewelry, finishing off the space with polish and flair. If you've chosen an eclectic style—or just want to add an eclectic element—knobs and pulls can put your unique stamp on the space.

UPDATE EXISTING CABINETRY FINISHES
FOR A NEW LOOK

ADD NEW HARDWARE

Fresh hardware can give a vanity an instant update. If you're not planning to refinish or reface, look for new pieces that will fit into or cover the existing hole spreads. (Pulls are sold with the inches or centimeters between the center of each post hole noted.) Choose new hardware to complement the lines and finishes of your faucets and installed accessories for a pulled-together look.

REFINISH IT

Another simple way to refresh a vanity is to refinish it. Bring a door to your local paint store to discuss ways to remove or cover the old paint or stain, and the best formulation for your bathroom. You can also add decorative elements like toekick valances, onlays, or legs at that point, ideally of the same material as the vanity if you're staining them.

Plug the holes where the original handles or knobs were placed if you want to change hardware configurations. Then give your vanity an entirely new look with a coat of paint or stain that complements the floor and countertop finishes.

REFACE IT

If you don't like the style of the doors and drawer fronts on your vanity, painting or staining them won't help. But refacing will. A professional refacing service or a DIY kit will provide a new veneer to cover any exposed sides, edges, or face frame components. It will also include matching doors and drawer fronts in your preferred new style and possibly decorative details to enhance the toekick or exposed side panels.

ABOVE New cabinet pulls can dress up the drawer fronts, be easier to grip with wet hands, and honor the traditional elements in the room. Their two-toned silver and black finish will also complement both the faucets and lights, which currently have no visual tie-in.

ABOVE The square legs on the outsides of the vanity add a delightful Arts and Crafts touch to its look, and would go even further in enhancing its style with complementary legs on the opposite sides. These can be constructed fairly easily from a well-matched wood and secured to the cabinet by a carpenter before painting.

TIME FOR A REDO?

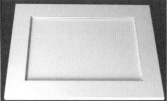

simply white
OC-117

ABOVE A creamy white coat of paint on the vanity and its new features will relieve the wooden monotony of the room and brighten the space. Always consult with a paint professional by bringing in an existing drawer front or door to get the best formulation for your project.

ABOVE The knotty slab drawer and door fronts on the vanity blend into the wood paneling on the walls and clash with the dressier faucets. The simplicity of refaced Shaker recessed fronts would pair well with the cabinet's legs and give this vanity an entirely new look.

LEFT You don't necessarily want to replace a vanity that's well constructed and offers ample storage drawers. But when it's not living up to the bathroom's style potential, there are ways to successfully update it with new looks and freshness.

medicine cabinets

● ● ● MEDICINE CABINETS HAVE BEEN A STANDARD feature in bathrooms going back several decades. They provide easy access to prescriptions and over-the-counter drugs as their name implies, but many occupants also use them for holding daily hygiene items. They provide a mirror on the outside of the door for grooming. Some higher-end models provide a second mirror on the back of the door, while other wider models provide triple mirrors for better side views.

Medicine cabinets may be recessed into a wall, surface-mounted against it, or partially recessed, with most of the depth in the wall cavity and a decorative frame or molding extending into the room. Some models offer a choice of surface or recessed mounting, and many have reversible hinges to accommodate mounting on a left or right side wall. There are also a few surface-mounted corner models on the market. The most widely available medicine cabinets are designed to fit between standard studs and are easy to replace later.

ABOVE Surface-mounted
medicine cabinets work well on
exterior walls, where it isn't always
possible to recess them. When
using one, it can be challenging to
find a wall light to install above it,
so a model with built-in lighting can
be a good option.

LEFT A medicine cabinet can add
style to a room, as well as storage.
A traditional recessed model with
inset door, crystal knob, and crown
molding carries through the vintage
theme embodied in the pedestal
sink below it.

FACING PAGE Medicine cabinets are traditionally hinged left or right,
depending on the room's architecture. Some new models have doors
that open upward, so that they don't interfere with pendant lights or
sconces next to them.

THE SMARTER MEDICINE CABINET

While some homeowners are forgoing medicine cabinets in favor of more integrated cabinetry, there are some enticing new offerings on the market worth considering.

Manufacturers are building entertainment features like TVs and sound systems that stream from your smart phone via Bluetooth into their new models. USB chargers for your devices are also available on some models, so you can safely store and power up your devices while in the bathroom.

More smart storage features being added to medicine cabinets include magnetic panels for holding small items like tweezers and nail clippers and lock boxes for prescription medicines.

Many also are integrating LED lighting into their mirrors. This helps with achieving the proper lighting levels for applying makeup. Some can be dimmed for a night-light effect, too.

ABOVE Your morning routine can be enhanced with your local traffic report and weather on a TV built right into your medicine cabinet. Or laugh along with your favorite late night host while you prepare for bed.

LEFT Medicine cabinets often store prescription drugs that can be dangerous in the wrong hands, especially those of curious children. A model with a lock box prevents accidents and theft, adding peace of mind and security to your private space.

LEFT Your medicine cabinet can help you get into your day more efficiently with organization elements for shaving, grooming, putting on makeup, and charging your devices, all in the same well-planned space.

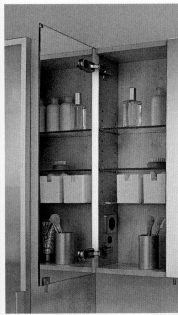

ABOVE Connectivity has come to the medicine cabinet with chargers and speakers that can stream your device's Bluetooth tunes or information programming.

additional bath storage

● ● ● THERE ARE MANY STORAGE OPTIONS FOR your bathroom beyond vanities and medicine cabinets. Shallow wall cabinets can be installed above the toilet to hold extra rolls of toilet tissue and other items. Tall shallow cabinets that hold smaller items can be recessed into unused wall space. Decorative items can be housed in open-front, recessed niches custom built for their display.

Tall linen cabinets can hold sheets and towels if you have the room. Roll-out trays improve accessibility in these deep spaces. If you lack floor or wall space for a traditional linen tower, you can store towels on floating shelves, in baskets, or in open wine-style storage on an available wall. Storage furniture is another option if you don't want to install more cabinets.

This bathroom adds storage behind hidden wall panels, making good use of space that would otherwise just be decorative. Instead, it packs considerable extra capacity for smaller items into recessed cabinetry.

LEFT Tall storage can make great use of limited floor space. Taking advantage of a high ceiling, a linen tower can hold items that won't fit into a vanity or don't need to be stored there.

ABOVE Not all of a bathroom's supplemental storage is built in. Freestanding items, like mobile carts, add capacity and flexibility. They can be easily added or moved, as needed, to meet changing demands.

LEFT Very small spaces require creative thinking when it comes to storage. Spaces that would otherwise go to waste, like those above doors or showers, can be harnessed for extra capacity. These out-of-regular-reach spots can be ideal for items not needed daily.

RIGHT Drawer dividers can make that key storage space perform far more efficiently. What might otherwise be a jumble of small items rolling around can become an organized stage for your daily routines instead.

ABOVE Storage accessories can greatly enhance the capacity of a cabinet. Door racks installed on the backs of doors create extra shelving for small items and put them within more convenient reach.

LEFT Until recently, many vanities lacked drawers because of the plumbing components within them. The U drawer, either included with a vanity or purchased and installed after, accommodates the plumbing and offers drawer storage around it. In many cabinets, it's possible to stack two of them to create drawers for two users.

ABOVE Pull-out accessories, long popular in kitchens, can bring better organization to your bathroom, as well. They work especially well at holding odd-shaped items that are harder to store in open cabinets or drawers.

RIGHT Tilt-out trays are another kitchen export that work exceptionally well in bathrooms. In addition to offering space for toothbrushes, floss, and toothpaste that would otherwise go unused behind a false panel, they can also hold a wedding ring safely away from a sink drain.

ADDING INTERIOR ACCESSORIES TO INCREASE STORAGE

n ot every vanity is blessed with drawers or interior accessories that maximize its storage capacity. That doesn't mean you're stuck with inferior storage. There are many options available on the market to enhance the cabinets you have, rather than having to replace them.

Maximize the open space. Rather than just pile items onto the floor of your vanity cabinets, consider a U drawer that wraps around the plumbing. Many vanities will accommodate two stacked U drawers, which can be very helpful in compact dual-occupant bathrooms.

Maximize your doors. There are organizers that attach to the inside of doors to hold hair dryers and other large items. These, too, take advantage of otherwise unused capacity. Swing-out trash cans are another option for door storage, as they hide your garbage and free up limited bathroom floor space.

Maximize dead space. Vanities often have false panels above the storage section. By adding a tilt-out tray kit this narrow space in front of the sink can be used to hold toothbrushes, floss, and other small grooming items. While most commonly used in kitchens, these trays can be very handy in bathrooms. Another kitchen accessory that works well in a bathroom is a tiered drawer organizer. This adds extra capacity for small items in tall vanity drawers.

vanity tops

● ● ● THERE IS A WIDE RANGE OF COUNTERTOP material options for bathroom vanities in just about every price point. Some are very low-maintenance and just require cleaning. Others require sealing and polishing. Some are extremely chip and scratch resistant. Others are easier to damage. Before selecting your countertop material, be sure you know its maintenance requirements and potential durability.

• engineered and natural stone

Stone tops may be natural, like onyx, granite, and marble. They also may be engineered, made mainly of quartz but compressed with resins to make them nonporous. Engineered stone tops are becoming the most popular countertop choice on the market today as they offer the durability of natural stone without its maintenance requirements.

• solid surface and composites

There are several categories of composites, ranging from affordable cultured marble to higher-end blends of concrete and jute. Solid surface (like the well-known Corian® brand) is often at a midrange price point. All of these materials are easy to maintain and offer varied looks. Many come with integral sinks for ease and style. Before deciding on a composite top, check with the manufacturer about its heat sensitivity. Otherwise, commonly used items like curling irons can damage your new surface.

• tile

Many older vanities are topped with tile. While generally durable, affordable, and easy to maintain, tile is also surrounded by grout, which can be difficult to keep stain-free over time. Traditionally, 3- or 4-inch tiles have been used for bathroom countertops, creating an ongoing chore for homeowners.

New porcelain slab and sintered compact surface technologies deliver the style options and durability of tile without grout. They also accommodate integral sinks.

Solid surface is another popular countertop choice for its soft matte finish, low-maintenance, repairability, and potential for an integral sink. Many builders put solid surface tops into their production homes in the '90s and last decade, as homeowners find them easy to live with.

RIGHT Tile tops fell out of favor due to the difficult job of maintaining their expansive grout. New thicknesses and formulations, including the addition of quartz in sintered compact surfaces, create long, strong slabs for a new breed of tile countertops.

BELOW For years, many equated granite with luxury, and it became a favorite countertop material in master bathrooms and powder rooms. It is highly durable and heat and scratch resistant, but does need to be sealed.

LEFT Engineered stone, also called quartz because of its major ingredient, is overtaking granite as the countertop of choice. Both offer excellent durability, but quartz doesn't require sealing. Its recently improved looks have overcome the main objection to using it in the past.

•laminate

Laminate offers affordability, easy DIY installation, and a wide range of looks that have greatly improved in recent years. It is widely available and easy to maintain, but also can be easy to damage and nonrepairable if cut, burned, or chipped. Also, in most cases, you will not be able to undermount a sink in laminate (though there are a few models and experienced installers who can make that happen).

•slab and recycled glass

Slab glass is an extremely durable and low-maintenance countertop that adds tremendous style and drama to a room. It also tends to be expensive, so you'll see it more often in compact powder rooms than in master or secondary baths. Some slab glass vanity tops are being made with integral sinks.

Recycled glass tops are typically compressed with a resin to create a stylish, dramatic counter. Most, but not all, need to be sealed.

•other materials

Vanity tops also can be wood, bamboo, copper, zinc, and other exotic materials. These offer a significant opportunity to add impact to a bathroom. It's important to know the properties and care of the material you're selecting. Many change colors over time if not exactly maintained while others can be damaged by water if not properly sealed.

ABOVE Recycled glass is another viable countertop material. Unlike the translucent tops, these are opaque, and take cast-off bottles, windows, and other glass sent to the recycling bin, combine it with binders, and compress it into slabs. Some are bound with concrete and need to be sealed; others use synthetic binders and don't need sealing.

LEFT Slab glass is a durable, low-maintenance, high-glamour material. Especially when lit from below, it creates a dramatic focal point in a bathroom.

Laminate is an affordable choice for bathrooms and comes in a myriad of styles to work with most projects. In recent years, new technologies have created more decorative edges for laminate tops and even the ability to undermount a sink in select offerings.

more about...
HOW TO CHOOSE A NEW TOP FOR YOUR EXISTING CABINETRY

new countertops can change the style of a bathroom tremendously, and can change how you use it, as well, depending on the type of material you choose.

Consider the material. Will the new countertop material add value to your home—as replacing a budget surface with an investment material like engineered stone, natural stone, or porcelain slab would? Will it be durable enough to last a decade or two without chipping or scratching? Will it offer low-maintenance and stain resistance? Does it make financial sense for your project and property? All of these considerations should go into your selection process.

Consider the look. When you've chosen the type of material you'll install, it's time to consider its appearance. Since it's going into an existing bathroom, you'll want to make sure that it will look good with the other surfaces in the room. Choose a color family that will complement the floor and wall surfaces (perhaps using one of their main colors), as well as the cabinetry. If both are heavily patterned, you might consider a solid color for the countertop. If the tile and cabinet are very simple, you can add drama with a more patterned and colorful countertop. To help users whose vision may be compromised, be sure there's a clear contrast between the cabinet, wall, and countertop colors.

Consider the add-ons. Your new countertops may not come with sinks. That will be a separate purchase to budget for. They may be thick enough to require faucet extenders. Will you need to purchase a backsplash and side splashes to cover walls damaged from removing the old splashes? Or will you be resurfacing the walls? All of these details need to be thought through when planning a countertop replacement.

floors, walls, windows, and doors

• • •

BEFORE YOU SOAK IN THE TUB OR WASH UP AT YOUR VANITY, YOU'VE surrounded yourself with your bathroom's walls, stepped on its floors, and probably came through a door. You may be enjoying light from a window or pulling down its shades for privacy. While the fixtures, cabinetry, and countertops may get most of your attention, your successful bathroom project begins with its architecture.

Your windows are likely to be the same types as those found elsewhere in your home for architectural consistency, as will doors that open to hallways and public rooms. It is not uncommon, though, to see a unique door used between the master bedroom and bathroom for style, functionality, or both.

There is a wide range of floor and wall options for bathrooms, and which one you choose will depend on how the space will be used, where it fits in the home's floor plan, and what investment level makes the most sense for your project.

Windows, doors, floors, and walls all play a major role in how your bathroom looks and functions. The tile floors and walls here are extremely durable and handle water well. The windows let light stream in and, with a private yard just beyond, can be kept uncovered. Only the window to the bedroom has a covering to provide light control and privacy.

A powder room or pool bath, for example, will often share the same wall coverings and flooring as the living spaces surrounding it. However, the pool bath's floor will need to be extremely moisture-friendly and slip-resistant to accommodate showering and feet wet from swimming.

Consider durability, maintenance, cost, style, and functionality—e.g., how the floor feels underfoot or whether a paint is scrubbable—when choosing floor and wall materials for your bathroom project.

wood, laminate, and bamboo floors

●●● WOOD, LAMINATE, AND BAMBOO FLOORING have become increasingly popular for bathroom projects, especially when they can extend into adjacent bedrooms and living spaces for a spacious, coordinated look. These materials should be professionally installed for the greatest longevity; improper installation can result in water penetration between the planks. Even with proper installation, it's best not to let water sit on these floors, or install them in a bathroom that will get a lot of spillover, like a child's bath. Wood floors with an oiled finish are especially susceptible to water damage and require regular refinishing.

Laminate is a practical, affordable, low-maintenance, durable alternative to wood floors that can work well in a half bath, especially when the flooring extends throughout the kitchen and living area, for cohesion. It is also DIY-friendly for someone with flooring skills and tools.

LEFT Wood flooring pairs well with this nautically inspired bathroom. Its blond planks evoke a ship's deck, but care is needed to protect it from shower spills.

BELOW Bamboo is another excellent wood alternative. It is a fast-growing sustainable grass that is water resistant with an attractive array of finishes. Be sure to research whether the product you're selecting is low in formaldehyde, as some low-cost imports have failed that indoor air quality standard.

porcelain, ceramic, and natural stone tile floors

● ● ● ONE OPTION FOR HOMEOWNERS WHO love the look of wood in the bathroom, but are concerned about its longevity there, is wood-look tile. The reproduction of natural wood on porcelain has gotten increasingly sophisticated. While it won't feel the same underfoot, it can definitely deliver the look.

Porcelain tile can also deliver natural stone looks for homeowners who don't want the expense, sealing, and polishing requirements of marble, limestone, and granite, but love their appearance. It is also easier and more affordable to install.

Another trend that has become popular with tile installations is larger tiles with rectified edges, which can be butted very tightly together for minimal grout. This creates a cleaner, more contemporary look that is also easier to maintain.

There is still the traditional ceramic tile option for anyone wanting a more affordable bathroom project. Tile is widely available and comes in a wide range of colors and patterns to create the look you want.

At the opposite end of the spectrum are natural stone tile floors. These are more complex—thus expensive—to install and will need to be sealed to prevent staining. Despite this, natural stone remains a popular choice for its innate beauty. If you're going to choose a polished stone like granite, it's worth having a professional apply antislip coating to reduce the chances of a fall.

RIGHT Tile has seen great improvements in printing and production capabilities. New offerings, especially from Europe, can duplicate natural stone, wood, or concrete looks without their maintenance requirements.

FACING PAGE, TOP Wood-look tile has exploded in popularity, thanks to its non-wood-like water friendliness, low-maintenance, and durability. It can extend throughout a master suite for greater cohesiveness, though it lacks wood's warmth underfoot.

FACING PAGE, BOTTOM Marble tile has been prized for its beauty and elegance since ancient times. It is still popular for master baths and powder rooms, though marble-look porcelain tile is gaining favor for its lower maintenance, lower price tag, and easier installation.

more about...
COORDINATING FLOORING WITH ADJACENT ROOMS

ven though bathrooms are private rooms, they usually relate to adjacent spaces, like a master bedroom or living area. You'll have a much more pulled-together space when the bathroom flooring complements that of its surrounding rooms.

Coordinate colors. Many homeowners enjoy the comfort of carpeting in their bedrooms, but it is not an ideal flooring for a bathroom. (A machine-washable bath mat can add the same softness to a bathroom without the mold or mildew risks.) To connect a master bath's flooring to the bedroom, consider choosing a color that matches closely to the carpeting, like light grey tile next to light grey carpeting. This will create a feeling of continuity in the suite and make both spaces feel larger. You can also do this with a bath that opens to a carpeted hallway.

Coordinate patterns. Sometimes you want more drama in a bathroom—especially a powder room or master bath—than you have in its neighboring spaces. To add that drama but also maintain the relationship between the two rooms, choose one of the dominant tones from the surrounding room's flooring to include in a pattern on the bathroom floor.

Extend materials. There are now floor tiles that look like wood that can extend from a bedroom or living area into a full bath, creating total style continuity. For a half bath, like a powder room, you can more easily continue wood, laminate, or other hard flooring.

other floor materials

●●● VINYL, LINOLEUM, AND CONCRETE ARE all options for bathroom floors. Sheet vinyl is a long-lasting and affordable choice, but should only be used in a bathroom without a barrier-free shower, and it should be professionally installed. There are also more DIY-friendly vinyl tiles and planks. Their wood and stone looks have gotten more realistic in recent years and they offer the advantages of easy maintenance, comfort underfoot, and antimicrobial properties. They should also be avoided in a bathroom with a barrier-free shower.

Linoleum is often confused with vinyl and also comes in sheets, planks, and tiles, but it's an all-natural product made from linseed oil. Like vinyl, it's antimicrobial and soft underfoot. It also is ideal for eco-conscious homeowners or those with respiratory issues. However, it is not a budget-level product and generally not waterproof, thus better for half baths than full.

Concrete is highly durable and water resistant, which makes it a good choice for pool baths, playroom baths, and outdoor master showers. It can be professionally finished to look like any material you choose, or custom-designed to create a completely personalized floor. People often think of concrete as an affordable option, but slabs are often discolored and damaged, thus requiring a new topcoat and professional refinishing, which can be very costly. Even with a finish, they need to be periodically resealed. This surface can get slick, and requires additives to make it nonslip. It is also very hard underfoot.

LEFT Linoleum, sold in sheets or individual tiles, is a sustainable flooring material perfect for half baths. It provides a soft surface ideal for aging-in-place projects and retro charm for transitional or traditional bathrooms.

FACING PAGE Concrete floors offer modern industrial style in their simplest, unadorned finish and are impervious to water or sand when sealed, making them ideal for coastal projects. They can also be personalized with highly decorative patterns and inset with objects like shells, stones, or fossils.

walls

●●●● IT'S NOT UNCOMMON IN BATHROOM remodels to change wall locations or configurations to create a better floor plan. Removing or shortening a wall can allow light from a water closet window to flow across the entire bathroom. Adding walls in an enlarged master bath can create dual water closets for increased privacy. Changing a standard wall to a thin partition may just add the inches necessary to meet code requirements to install a double vanity next to an existing toilet.

In many areas of the world where space is strictly limited, toilet room walls are constructed of shower glass by the shower door contractor. Sandblasting, etching, or films create privacy.

You'll also be deciding on your wall finishes and coverings in a bathroom addition or remodel. Those choices will depend on practical considerations, like how much water they'll be exposed to, how easy or difficult they'll be to clean, and what other maintenance requirements may be involved (like sealing or polishing), before you decide on color and pattern.

Sometimes you don't have the inches to build a standard privacy wall for a toilet and still meet code. In those situations, a narrow partition wall can work well. It can also allow light from a nearby window to reach other parts of the room and add a decorative element.

It's not uncommon to find multiple materials on a wall, most often tile and paint. The tile provides a water-friendly backsplash for sinks, but needn't be limited to just the inches above the countertop. The full-height treatment in this bathroom creates a practical focal point for the vanity elements.

Mirrors can provide the illusion of spaciousness in a smaller bathroom. While traditionally used just over a vanity, they can extend throughout the room, offering full-length, multiperspective views while getting dressed.

•wall tile options

One of the most popular wall covering options for bathrooms is tile. There is a tremendous range of choices, from affordable ceramic to elegant, upscale marble. Many designers and homeowners are choosing porcelain tile that looks like marble for its lower cost and maintenance.

Glass and metal tile are popular dramatic accents. Mosaics, now typically mesh-mounted on sheets for easier installation, are also a popular style choice for adding interest to bathroom walls. These tiny tile pieces add great beauty, but also increased upkeep with all that extra grout.

The latest trend coming out of Europe looks like mosaics, but is actually a single large tile inkjet-printed and dimensioned to look like tiny pieces. You'll get all the style but with less grout to maintain and faster installation.

ABOVE Tiles with dimensionality add interest to a wall. They come in different styles to create different looks, from pop art to sophisticated texture. While adding a unique statement to a wall, they can also add time and effort to your maintenance, so be sure to do your research before buying.

LEFT Glass mosaics add shimmering beauty to a bathroom project. There is a tremendous range of sizes, colors, and finishes to choose from, so you can create exactly the look you want. One especially popular effect is the blue-green blend for coastal charm.

BELOW Glass tile comes in many shapes, allowing you to create different looks in your bathroom. One oft-chosen option is subway tile, evoking the old-world look of that shape, but elevating it above the standard ceramic.

LEFT Mosaics have been popular for thousands of years, but have gotten a twenty-first century update with new production technologies. The latest innovation is a large tile with dimensional printing that looks like mosaics, but is as simple to install as any other field tile. It also requires minimal grout lines around the large tiles only, rather than between each mesh-mounted tiny tile, greatly reducing maintenance.

PORCELAIN WALL SLABS AND
SISTERED COMPACT SURFACES

Large, thin porcelain tile slabs have emerged in recent years as a stylish, low-maintenance wall covering that can handle moisture and daily use. Most of these are from Italy and Spain, where the factories have gotten increasingly sophisticated in producing natural stone and wood looks on tiles exceeding 5 by 10 feet. Some of these slabs offer book matching, so that the pattern on one slab matches up to the pattern on the adjacent slab. This provides a more natural look across an entire wall, and is especially popular for marble-look tile.

With proper substrate preparation, these tiles can be butted up to each other for joints as tight as $1/16$ inch, making for tremendously easy cleaning. They're also extremely thin and light, despite their strength, which means an easier installation.

Porcelain slab can be carried from the walls onto tub surrounds and vanities for design continuity in a modern bath. Here, the black floor and wall tile sets off the marble and updates its traditional appeal.

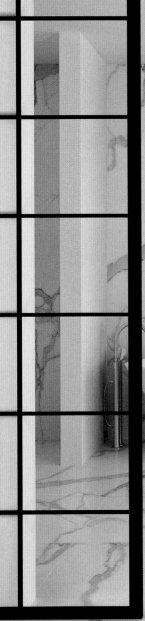

LEFT Porcelain manufacturers can now reproduce marble looks in large slabs that deliver the look without the upkeep or massive installation cost.

BELOW While natural stone has dominated the porcelain slab category, it's not the only style available. Wood-looks, also a popular porcelain application, have gotten slab treatment for wall cladding. This creates a new option for shower surrounds, too.

RIGHT These oversize tiles are ideal for wall surfaces in wet and dry areas of a bathroom. They can go straight into a shower, if desired, as easily as a deep windowsill. They're versatile enough to work in a contemporary, traditional, or eclectic space.

•other wall covering options

There are many other coverings for bathroom walls. Paint and wallpaper are popular and affordable choices for walls that won't get wet. Either can completely change the style of a room in a weekend, but both require skill to achieve a professional look. Paint is easier to change, and is often the first choice for homeowners who don't plan to keep their home for long. Mirroring an entire wall of a small bath is another affordable option that will add drama and make the room feel more spacious, but it requires regular upkeep to remove smudges.

Wood tiles or paneling are also versatile options that can add either a traditional, modern, or rustic look, depending on the finish chosen. They should not be used where they will be in direct contact with water. They can be installed partially up the wall as wainscoting, with paint or wallpaper continuing to the ceiling. Tile wainscoting is also often combined with paint or paper.

BELOW Mirrored walls visually expand a space and amplify other cladding and light with their reflections. However, they do require more work to keep them smudge-free.

LEFT Wood wainscoting is often stained or painted white, but needn't be. A pop of color can add unexpected whimsy to a room. Here pink provides a lovely backdrop to a Venetian-style mirror and pedestal sink.

ABOVE Wood has traditionally been used in bathrooms as full paneling or partial wainscoting. A newer application is wood tiles. These add dramatic beauty to a bath project, but should be kept to dry spaces only. A powder room focal point wall would be an ideal use.

LEFT Wallpaper is another traditional wall covering, and provides a low-maintenance surface with color and pattern. Rather than cover an entire bathroom in it, wallpaper can be used for just one focal-point wall, as is done here to enhance the tub area.

bathroom redo & reuse

UPDATE YOUR BATHROOM WALLS

S ometimes your bathroom walls are covered in peeling wallpaper or an unattractive, damaged mirror. Sometimes they're clad in ugly wall tile whose grout has seen better days. If you're lucky, your walls just need a new coat of paint. Fortunately, your bathroom's surfaces can typically be updated in a few weekends with hired help or sweat equity.

NEW PAINT

A fresh coat of paint is the easiest, most dramatic, and least expensive change you can make to your walls. If they were previously covered in glass, paper, plaster, paneling, or tile, you will have some prep work to do to the wall before you can successfully paint. Look for a color that will complement the room's style and other finishes and consult with your local paint source for the formulation that will work best for your room.

NEW TILE

Tile is one of the most versatile and livable surfaces you can apply to your bathroom walls, but replacing old with new is a messy and challenging job. Choosing the new tile doesn't have to be, though. Select colors, shapes, and patterns that will coordinate with the other tiles and finishes in the room, and use it to create an updated focal point at the same time.

NEW MIRROR

You can replace your old mirror or give it a new look with a frame kit. Frame kits can be tricky to install if your mirror extends all the way into a corner and down to your backsplash. (Sometimes frames can be too large to fit between the wall and a side wall medicine cabinet.) Professional glass framers can be helpful if you do have the space, but the cost can be relatively high.

Another option is to carefully remove the existing mirror, refinish the wall behind it, and choose a framed mirror to update the room. Find a frame that matches the cabinetry or one that will complement its style and color in a fresh, interesting material.

RIGHT Sometimes a bath just needs some added oomph even if there's nothing fundamentally wrong with its style or functionality. That's an easy update, fortunately, with new wall treatments that will enhance the room's Arts and Crafts style.

TOP A natural framed mirror can add a new texture to the sink wall. Although it won't be as large as the existing mirror, it can definitely provide far more style and interest, while still doing its job of facilitating bathroom grooming.

ABOVE LEFT Paint is one of the easiest and most affordable elements of a room to change. A period-friendly shade of green would add a deeper, richer hue to the room, while honoring its overall look.

ABOVE RIGHT One of the room's weakest features is its basic beige tile wainscot. Replacing that with an updated, still historic-inspired, hexagon tile will do two things. First, it creates more interest on the walls. Second, its darker shades better complement the existing floor.

doors

●●● THERE ARE SEVERAL FACTORS TO CONSIDER when choosing a door for your bathroom. How much light and sound does it need to block? Hollow-core doors, which are among the most common, tend to allow more noise transfer. Framed frosted glass and louver doors are popular for their style, but allow more light penetration.

Solid wood doors offer excellent light and noise blocking but tend to be very expensive. They can also be damaged by excess moisture if too close to the tub or shower. Solid core doors can be a more affordable choice.

In addition to choosing your door's material, you will also be choosing its type. The standard is a single door that swings into the bathroom. While offering affordability and wide selection, this door also limits floor space to accommodate its swing. A wider bathroom entry might require a double swing (French) door, but these often open into larger baths with entry halls.

Where space is at a premium, a pocket door that slides into the wall when open is an excellent option as it allows better use of the floor space. It isn't always possible, however, to install one. To achieve the benefits of a pocket door where one can't be installed, a sliding door on an exterior track—often called a barn door—is an alternative. You'll need adjacent wall space for it to rest when open and room above for the track.

Master bathroom doors should be chosen to complement the space, as well as meet their essential role. This traditional-style door works well in this cheery space.

LEFT Projects that include wet rooms need doors that are water-tolerant. These may be traditional or glass walls with swinging doors or even barn-door-style with water-friendly track, hardware, and handles.

ABOVE Barn doors roll on a track above the door opening and work well in spaces where a traditional swing could take up too much room. They're also used where a pocket door isn't possible because of mechanical elements in the wall. They do need sufficient space to rest when open though.

LEFT Indoor-outdoor living has made the concept of a wall that fully opens popular. This is generally achieved with door panels that open and stack against a side wall accordion-style. Burying the track in the floor so that bare feet don't have to strike against raised cold, hard metal is the optimum installation.

floors, walls, windows, and doors 167

windows

• • • A BATHROOM BENEFITS GREATLY FROM THE natural light windows let in. While not always possible, when planning an addition, attic conversion, or basement bathroom, take every opportunity to include windows in your plans.

There are different types of windows to pair with different architectural styles. It's best to choose one for your bath conversion or addition that is compatible with the other windows in your home. They might be casement windows that hinge left or right, double-hung that open up (the most common style), sliders that open across each other, bifold that stack open, jalousie or awning windows that open out, or fixed windows (like stained glass or glass block) that don't open at all.

Privacy is a major concern for bathroom windows, and can be addressed by the window itself or how it's covered. Glass block and frosted glass will allow light through, while obscuring views into the room. Stained glass will also provide privacy, but can reduce light penetration, depending on the design. Another privacy option if you're changing your windows is to select models that have blinds sandwiched between glass panes. Though these can be expensive and difficult to get repaired if damaged, they are another option for water-friendly window coverings.

BELOW Double-hung windows are among the most common found in American homes. These open on tracks and allow fresh air in. Arched windows are often used for decoration above them, and are most frequently nonoperable.

Energy efficiency is another consideration when you're choosing new windows. Energy Star ratings will tell you how a window will perform in your climate, so you don't need to become an expert on low-e ratings, glazing types, or different gas fills that can help you reduce your heating or cooling bills. Typically, the better its rating, the more you'll pay for the window, so how long you'll remain in the house and how much you can save on your utility bills will be important considerations in choosing your new windows.

LEFT While some bathrooms offer a wall of doors for access to the outside, others offer a wall of windows to enjoy the view. These provide a luxury amenity to a master bathroom, and their elevated location allows for privacy without window coverings.

ABOVE Casement windows that open to the left or right, rather than up, are an alternative to double-hung windows. They may also be installed next to nonoperable picture windows to create a wall of glass.

RIGHT A window can provide natural, ambient light to a room, as well as a lovely view for a tub user. The large picture window in this bathroom provides a peek into a private garden. Because that area is solely used by the master suite and is surrounded by a high fence, the windows to it do not need to be covered.

light, heat, and ventilation

● ● ●

IMAGINE YOURSELF STEPPING OUT OF YOUR SHOWER OR TUB INTO AN unheated, unventilated, dark bathroom—probably how your great-great-great-grandparents did once upon a time. Fortunately, even the smallest bathrooms today have heat, ventilation, and light. And they are far more sophisticated than ever.

Bathroom lighting has become much more complex in recent years, especially in large master suites. No longer is a four-bulb light bar at the vanity mirror and a single recessed light above the shower considered sufficient for a larger room.

While you'll find more multifaceted lighting systems being designed into bathrooms today, you'll also come up against more stringent energy use codes for planning them. If the bathroom lighting is not high efficacy (LED or fluorescent for lower wattage requirements), many municipalities require an occupancy sensor as the main control. This has driven the development of lighting technology that delivers both illumination and low power demands.

Ventilation is essential, too. It ensures that the air you breathe is fresh, whether it's coming from a fan, an open window, or both. A poorly ventilated bathroom is at much greater risk of developing mold problems, which can be extremely dangerous.

Heating keeps you comfortable, especially when you're wet. Be sure to factor it into your bathroom project so that it's as inviting as the rest of your home. It will either be tied into your home's central heating system or something added just for that space, like radiant floor heat.

Bathroom lighting has evolved a long way from builder-grade light bars above a vanity mirror. New task lighting options include sconces or pendants, but sunshine streaming through a window or skylight is always a beneficial ambient light feature.

lighting types

●●● LIGHTING SHOULD BE PLANNED IN LAYERS with ambient light illuminating the entire space, task lights focusing on key areas, night-lights providing safety and comfort, and even accent lighting playing up key features.

• ambient lighting

Ambient light most often comes from recessed ceiling lights. Master baths may include decorative lighting fixtures like chandeliers, but code restrictions for such lighting exist to avoid fatal shocks when standing in a tub.

The most natural ambient light comes from the sun, which may shine into your bathroom through windows or standard or tubular skylights. Both skylight types—the large familiar rectangular and newer smaller tubes—can greatly enhance your space with warmth and brightness. The standard skylight is expensive to purchase, install, and maintain. This has led to the development of tubular skylights, which require a much smaller hole in your roof.

• task lighting

Vanities once lit mainly by light bars might now get pendants or sconces instead. Sconces and pendants should be installed with the users' height in mind to best illuminate their faces.

Task lighting might also be installed inside cabinets to make it easier to see their contents. Task lighting above the shower makes bathing easier.

• accent lighting

Accent lighting in bathrooms may take the form of a lighting strip below a floating vanity, along its facade, or in the toekick of a standard cabinet to provide night-lighting. It may also be tucked behind a ceiling detail to cast a soft glow. Accent lighting may even come installed in an upscale tub or showerhead as chromatherapy lighting.

TOP Accent lighting on cabinetry works well as night-lighting when the room is dark. It can also help you find contents in the drawer when the room lights are off.

RIGHT The most common sources of ambient light are clear window panes. The ones shown here fit into doors that open to the outside. In a country setting without immediate neighbors, they can remain uncovered.

LEFT Skylights are an alternative to windows for bringing daylight into a room. Some are operable, allowing for fresh air to ventilate the space, as well. They are more expensive to install and maintain than tubular versions.

BELOW LEFT Tubular skylights are a practical alternative to larger, standard skylights. They look like recessed lights but offer the benefits of natural light otherwise unavailable to an interior bathroom.

BELOW RIGHT Task lighting for vanities is an opportunity to add style to a room, as well as effective illumination. These mirror-flanking sconces will offer flattering light to someone using the sink much more than a light bar above it would.

THE NEW LEDS

When LEDs (light-emitting diodes) first emerged in the marketplace as an energy-efficient alternative to incandescent lighting and even compact fluorescents, they were not attractive, easily available, or affordable enough for most homes. They have come a long way since then and offer a greater selection of colors, temperatures (i.e., how warm or cool the light is), sizes, styles, and price points. Increasingly stringent energy codes have definitely sped their development and acceptance.

LEDs have also evolved into new shapes, including light strips built right into mirrors, medicine cabinets, and vanity fronts; recessed lights so compact that their trims nearly disappear into the ceiling; and LED-powered pendants, sconces, light bars, and chandeliers with tremendous style.

No longer cold, LEDs now have a much more natural glow for residential bathrooms. They are now also fully dimmable, which is ideal for a layered lighting plan. However, since LEDs dim differently than incandescent lights, it's best to see the fixture you're considering dimmed before specifying it for your project.

ABOVE Bath bars have been a fixture in houses for decades. They've improved in style over the years and, more recently, in energy efficiency. LED fixtures make bath bars much more economical to light your vanity area than incandescents, and they last longer than compact fluorescents.

RIGHT Sconces installed on the sides of mirrors offer more flattering light than fixtures mounted above. The increasing availability of LED-illuminated sconces offers more energy-efficient options to homeowners.

LEFT Decorative fixtures like chandeliers and pendants are increasingly making their way into luxury bathrooms. This one illuminates a focal point freestanding tub with LED illumination.

BELOW Recessed cans are another way to provide ambient light to a room. They're also another type of fixture that has seen LED capacity begin to dominate. The reason is that many rooms—including large masters—have more than one and need to meet local energy codes. LEDs make that possible.

UPDATE YOUR BATH WITH NEW VANITY AREA LIGHTING

bathrooms often suffer from poor and unattractive lighting. Your bathroom might have a bare bulb light bar over your mirror or down its sides. If your home was built more recently, it may have a small fixture above each sink that barely supplies enough light to read a prescription label. Keep in mind that replacing old fixtures using existing wiring is a simpler project than running wires to a new fixture.

REPLACE OLD VANITY LIGHTS

An updated fixture can provide new style to a dated vanity area. It can also provide added functionality with more light or positioning options, if that fits your space and style. By using energy efficient LEDs, you likely won't exceed the capacity of the existing wiring.

ADD A RECESSED LIGHT IN THE CEILING

You can also add light to a vanity area by adding a recessed ceiling light, ideally LED. Putting the new light on a separate switch gives you flexibility in how much light is available for each task. This is usually a job for a licensed electrician.

UPDATE RELATED LIGHT FIXTURES

Your bathroom may have additional ceiling or wall lights that share the same style as the fixtures you're replacing at the vanity. This is a good time to replace those, as well, for updated style and energy efficiencies. You may not be able to find something from the same series, but coordinating styles that share shapes and colors can work just as well, and can even add interest.

FAR LEFT It's not uncommon to find that a manufacturer has discontinued the series you bought in past years. It's perfectly acceptable to find a coordinating fixture, rather than an exact match. Look for complementary details and finishes—like the polished chrome and white glass here—to make the new work with the old.

TOP LEFT A new angled sconce updates the room's style and offers energy savings through its LED capability. While working with the traditional character of the room's fixtures and faucets, it freshens the space with a more transitional look.

BOTTOM LEFT A dark bathroom can benefit from the added illumination of a recessed can light. It will need to handle moisture for a room with a shower or tub, and it will ideally be small to minimize ceiling cutting. An LED fixture, rather than an incandescent one, will require far less energy to run.

TIME FOR A REDO?

Even a historically inspired bathroom can get a lighting modernization. Keeping with the style of the room, you can still add functionality and energy efficiency. And by not relocating fixtures, your installation costs are reduced.

heating

● ● ● IN NO OTHER ROOM IS HEATING AS essential as it is in a full bathroom, where a user is likely to be both naked and wet on a regular basis. Getting out of a shower or tub or even just stepping barefoot onto a tiled bathroom floor can be a chilling experience—especially in colder seasons—and the bathroom's heating system needs to offset this as quickly and efficiently as possible. Fortunately, there are several excellent options available to heat this space in conjunction with your home's central heating system or on their own.

In many American homes, a central gas, solar, or electric-powered heating system provides basic comfort for a dressed user and for a smaller bathroom. During a remodel these can be supplemented with a radiant floor heating system installed in the bathroom floor. Newer offerings allow you to install conductive mat systems below your flooring surface and operate them on their own controls. The mats heat up the flooring and the flooring heats up the room. Some new models can be programmed from your smart phone. Be sure to talk with your flooring and radiant system suppliers to make sure the combination is workable. Not all flooring materials are ideally suited for this purpose.

Some bathrooms add heat through an integrated fan/heat/light fixture that serves multiple purposes. These are often installed near the shower to avoid that pre-dry-off chill. Be sure to consult with an electrician as a new heating system, even one combined with a vent fan, could require a new dedicated circuit.

Radiant floor heating is an increasingly popular add-on for cold-climate bathrooms. New installation systems make it practical to use in a single room and control with its own panel. Some are now operable by smart phone apps to warm up before you start your day and cool down as you pull out of the driveway.

LEFT Some larger master bathrooms have added heating features of their own. One option is a discreet heater tucked below a floating vanity. This can definitely take the chill off a late-night bathroom visit.

ABOVE Having an effective heating system makes it far more comfortable to exit a steam shower and dry off at a leisurely pace. This enhances the overall experience of enjoying your new master bathroom.

water heaters

●●● HEATING A HOME'S WATER CAN CONSUME a significant portion of its energy costs, so it's important to plan carefully. Some remodeling projects can take advantage of the existing system, but if you're adding a tub or multiple showerheads where none existed before, it is important to review whether the current capacity will meet the new demand.

Many bathroom additions require an expansion of your water heating system. In some cases, a larger tank can replace the existing model and meet the need. In other instances, especially with room additions and attic or basement conversions, a supplement is required. Tankless water heaters are often used to meet this need.

Also called a demand or instantaneous heater, a tankless water heater doesn't store and constantly heat water, so it can be an energy-efficient add-on. It will cost more than a standard hot water storage model, but it can last longer and will hit your utility bills less. Tankless heaters can be gas- or electric-powered, depending on what's available in your area. They are also Energy Star-rated, so you can gauge how much they'll impact your utility bills.

ABOVE New large soaker tubs can take your current water heater beyond its capacity. It's just as important to plan ahead for how you'll heat your remodeled bathroom's water as it is to heat the room itself.

LEFT Showers with multiple heads and jets can also tax your water heating system, even with recent water conservation codes. When planning one of these popular features into your project, factor in additional capacity so that your user experience is everything you want it to be.

FACING PAGE When planning a new bathroom—especially one with a tub or shower in an attic or basement—it's essential to consider how you'll bring heat to the space so that it's as comfortable to use as the rest of your home.

ventilation

• • • EFFECTIVE BATHROOM VENTILATION IS essential for your health, especially in spaces with tubs and showers. Without it, harmful or even deadly mold can develop. Good ventilation will also pull unpleasant odors from the room, which is why you'll find vent fans even in windowless half baths.

Depending on the size and layout of your bathroom, you may need more than one exhaust fan. Separate water closets without operable windows and steam showers should have their own, for example.

There are codes and guidelines on how much capacity is needed. Ventilation is measured in cubic feet per minute, commonly called CFM. While a standard 5-foot by 8-foot bathroom would seem to require just 40 CFM, the minimum recommendation is 50. Ventilation for larger bathrooms can be determined by the number of fixtures. The Home Ventilating Institute (HVI) suggests 50 CFM minimum each for toilet, shower, and soaking tub, but 100 CFM for a jetted tub.

Your bathroom will also need a source of make-up air for the humid air that's pulled out. This can come from an open window or operable skylight, or from the space between the door and threshold. There should be at least ¾ inch of space for a windowless room.

FAR LEFT There are now vent fans on the market that can bring your smart phone's music or programming into the room, along with fresh air. They pair with your phone's Bluetooth so that the phone can stay safe and dry in a nearby room while you get ready for work.

LEFT A humidity-sensing fan turns on and off automatically based on need. This can be ideal for those who are memory-challenged, whether they're distracted teenagers or seniors. The room stays comfortable, the air stays safe, and your energy bills stay low.

FACING PAGE The original ventilation system—an operable window—still works well for moving fresh air into a bathroom and stale air out. However, an open window is far less comfortable in cold weather, so a supplemental vent fan is helpful in less hospitable climates.

ENHANCING YOUR BATH WITH A BETTER VENT FAN

Ventilation is one of the most important components of a bathroom and a good quality vent fan can really enhance your room's comfort, safety, and appeal. One of the reasons vent fans are so often left off when they should be used is noise. Another reason is that the user forgets to turn the fan on. Both of these reasons can be overcome with an upgraded model.

Improve operation. In order for a vent fan to do its job, it needs to be operating. A moisture-sensing model can turn on automatically when it senses humidity in a full bath and turn off when the humidity has been removed. These can be ideal in bathrooms for teens, children, or seniors where there may be a tendency to forget to turn a fan on or off. Many municipalities now require vent fans to have humidity sensors, so be sure to check if this is the case for your area. If not, a motion-sensing model could also work. Some fans combine both options.

Add features. There are many vent fans on the market that will also heat and light a bathroom. They tend to have a similar appearance to standard models, though there are a few that look more like standard lights. New vent fans on the market will not only pull fouled air out of the room, but can also stream your music or podcasts via Bluetooth.

Enhance your experience. Whichever features you decide on, whether for convenience, comfort, or entertainment, one you want to be sure to include is quiet. The HVI recommends a maximum noise rating of 1 sone or less, the equivalent of a refrigerator. Anything louder is disruptive.

entertainment, electronics, and extras

9

• • •

WHAT DEFINES BASIC FUNCTIONALITY AND LUXURY SHIFTS WITH EACH generation, and bathroom features shift along with them. Many of the high-tech innovations in this chapter would have been unthinkable extravagances in the past, but now they are becoming more common and soon might even be thought of as standard. And as our lives have become more high-tech-oriented, so have our homes. Nowhere is this seen more than in our personal electronics. Smart phones go everywhere with us, including into the bathroom. Being connected to the world, be it through TV, radio, or our connected devices, has also extended into our private spaces.

Most of these upgrades would be made to the master suite, but if your kids are carrying the phones you bought them into the bathroom while getting ready for school or bed, it's worth considering some options for protecting your electronic investment there, too.

Well-appointed master bathrooms may also include a television, home automation features, coffeemaker and other comforts, as well as conveniences usually found elsewhere in the home. A luxurious master suite may function like a small apartment with its own laundry closet, exercise area, and minikitchen, with some of those features moving into the traditional bathroom space.

Master bathrooms have gotten more bells and whistles, along with increased square footage. It's not uncommon to find a towel warmer, sound systems, and other living-space amenities in new construction and remodeled projects.

hot trend
THE WIRED MASTER BATH

One of the main reasons homeowners want to bring their devices into the bathroom is to enjoy their news, music, or entertainment. However, that puts these delicate electronics at risk of water damage. There are alternatives, like Bluetooth-enabled showerheads and vent fans that keep your device in a safe dry spot while you enjoy your podcast or music in the shower. Either is a fairly simple replacement for an existing fixture.

There are more elaborate options, too, like a mirror or medicine cabinet with a charger and speakers or television built in. Those will require more professional help in wiring the room for their power and connections.

Room lighting, climate, privacy through automated window coverings, and sound also are getting automated for bathrooms. Many of them can be controlled from a smart phone or tablet, or from sleek wall controls. All of these sophisticated systems can meet twenty-first-century needs while turning your bathroom into a spa-friendly environment.

ABOVE The basic switch has been transformed with control panels—or smart phone apps—that operate lights, temperature, window coverings, and security, combining all of these features in sleek, user-friendly interfaces.

LEFT Window coverings can now be operated from your phone, or on a wall-mounted control panel. In situations where a window is above a large tub or high out of reach, this automation allows you to enjoy your privacy with greater convenience.

RIGHT Your shower can now stream your smart phone's tunes or podcasts via Bluetooth, along with your water. This can make getting ready in the morning, or getting ready for bed, a more enjoyable or informative experience.

BELOW Television screens can be built into most mirrors by specialized firms, or be purchased that way from a manufacturer. The choice you make will be determined by the style you're creating in the space.

televisions

●●● PERHAPS YOU SEE YOURSELF ENJOYING your favorite show while soaking in a bubble bath. Or you want to catch up on local news and traffic while you get ready for work. If your master bath has a comfortable lounge area, you might even enjoy *Masterpiece Theater* with a glass of wine before ending your evening.

How you wish to enjoy your programming will have a significant impact on where you place the TV. Unless it's outdoor-rated, you definitely want it out of the range of tub splashing or shower spray. This could be on a direct view wall across the room. TV viewing from a bathtub, which is often the chosen placement, means looking up at a screen, possibly far up the wall and fairly close. A mount that lets it angle down toward the viewer can be helpful. A flexible mount that lets you reposition the screen for different areas can also work well.

In some instances, you don't want to see the TV at all when it's not in use. There are models that disappear from view when they're not being used, either tucked into a cabinet or sliding behind a piece of art. Or you could use a motorized mount within a piece of furniture or a cabinet.

There are also televisions built into vanity mirrors or medicine cabinets designed for stand-up viewing. While many are small to allow you to see more of your reflection while applying cosmetics or shaving, some manufacturers are making screens up to 27 inches that disappear when turned off.

Televisions are even making their way into lavish traditional bathrooms. They will sometimes be installed on a heavy-duty mount that can be turned in different directions for viewing from different areas of the bathroom.

Many homeowners want to enjoy their favorite shows while bathing. This will often entail mounting a television fairly high and possibly angled down toward the tub. Planning such an installation takes specialized knowledge and experience, usually with a home entertainment consultant.

more about...
SOUND SYSTEMS

(i) f you've created a luxurious master suite with a bathroom designed for lengthy visits, you'll want to enjoy your music there. There are water-tolerant in-ceiling or in-wall speakers that will bring your favorite composers into the bath, while being fairly minimalist. If you're building an addition or doing an extensive remodel, the speakers can be factored into a larger entertainment system.

If you don't want to invest in a built-in sound system for your bathroom, finding a discreet spot for a high-quality Bluetooth-enabled speaker can meet your needs. Be sure to check its water tolerance, however, before bringing it into a space where it might get splashed.

There are now even speakers built directly into spa tubs or medicine cabinets. These are often controlled by your smart phone or tablet, so it's important to find a place in the room where they can be used without the risk of getting wet.

LEFT A vanity mirror installation may facilitate TV viewing only from that location. If you want to watch while bathing or relaxing in a chair, you'll need to check your sightlines and potentially consider a different placement strategy.

UPDATE YOUR BATH WITH DIY DIGITAL ENHANCEMENTS

Old bathrooms can learn new tricks. Smart phone technology allows you to add automated features that once required a specialized consultant. You can now affordably add luxuries like automated lights, window coverings, and built-in smart phone chargers to keep your devices safe in the bathroom.

AUTOMATE YOUR LIGHTS

If you want to operate your lights using smart controls on your digital devices, you can now install a system to do this on your own. These new systems by several manufacturers don't require changes to your electrical system, but tap into them electronically. There are online tutorials and help desks to guide you through setting them up.

AUTOMATE YOUR WINDOW COVERINGS

This may seem like a luxury, but if your window is high above a tub or shower, being able to operate the shade without stepping in is a nice feature. You'll be limited to the looks provided by the manufacturer, but you'll enjoy more control and convenience. Motorized shades are now available in battery-operated options up to 12 feet wide, so you don't have to work with your home's wiring. These shades also can be tied to timers that meet your schedule and privacy needs.

STAY IN CHARGE

Many device owners have learned the hard way that water and cell phones don't mix well. Bathrooms can become a danger zone for your electronics. Chargers built into drawers or medicine cabinets can keep them safe and dry while you're bathing or filling your sink for a shave.

LEFT Smart phone chargers are increasingly found in bathroom storage. One of the simplest to add is a drawer-based system, which can also accommodate other needs. Be sure to check into whether a GFCI rating is required for your location, depending on its proximity to water.

TIME FOR A REDO?

LEFT Even a handsomely updated bathroom can benefit from some new twenty-first-century innovations. Automation can simplify life for its users, and finding a place to safely store and charge one's devices away from sink and shower is a smart strategy.

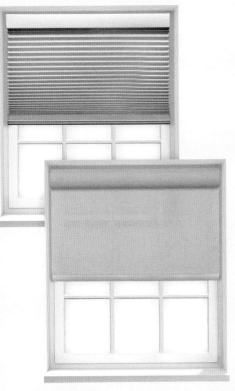

TOP Being able to cover the window high on the wall, and then easily operate that covering, can be a benefit to anyone whose bath is open to the bedroom, or whose home sits next to a taller neighbor. A smart phone app or wall control can make room darkening and privacy as easy as a click of the finger.

ABOVE There are homeowners who don't know how to operate their thermostats after living in a home for years. A new automated system lets you adjust a room's temperature easily and intuitively. You can also adjust lighting and turn your security system on and off with many models. Smart phone apps simplify the process even more.

decorative touches

● ● ●

DECORATIVE TOUCHES CAN ADD STYLE AND PERSONALITY TO YOUR bathroom project. They also can update a tired room without requiring a remodel or contractor. Details like window treatments, shower curtains, even vanity accessories and towels can really impact a bathroom's overall appearance with minimal effort and expense.

When choosing the different elements that will complete your bath project, it's important to keep several factors in mind. First, will the material make sense for the space and user? For example, a glass vanity set would be problematic in a children's bath because of possible breakage. One made of stainless steel or resin would be better suited.

Second, will the style of the new item mesh well with the existing finishes and forms in the room? It's great to update a space with noninstalled elements, but they should be added to complement and freshen their surroundings.

Last, but definitely not least, will the care required for your decorative elements take too much of your time or budget? For example, a fine, dry-clean-only Persian rug may dress up your traditional bathroom beautifully, but if it can't be easily spot-cleaned when you drop toothpaste or nail polish on it, it might work better elsewhere in your home.

The window shutters, artwork, tissue box cover, and shells sitting on the vanity all reinforce the room's relaxed coastal style. They also beautifully complement the soft finishes, like the wall paint, wood floor, and stone top, creating a casually elegant bathroom.

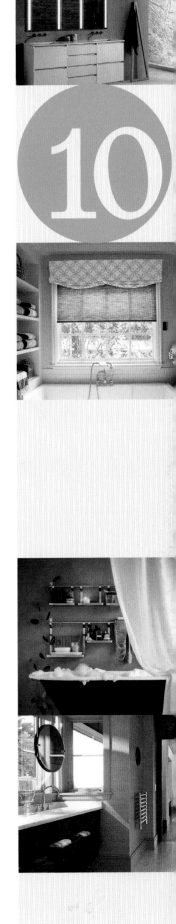

built-ins

●●● SOME LARGER BATHROOMS ARE BLESSED with built-in furniture. This could be a window seat made from a dormer or bay window that provides a comfortable lounging spot. Or it could be a built-in designed for display, like a row of niches to showcase a collection. Built-in cubbies to hold extra towels are another popular option.

Built-ins need to be planned into your new construction or remodeling project. Be sure to include both the space needed to comfortably and safely use the built-in and sufficient floor space in front to approach it. A display niche can be created at any height and location but should be accessible for placement, removal, and cleaning, while towel storage should be within easy reach. If you're going to light a display cabinet, planning needs to be factored in for the wiring and power source, as well.

FAR LEFT This handsome decorative shelving unit, made from the same wood as the cabinetry and green glass, serves two roles. First, it creates a room divider that provides some privacy for the toilet. Second, it serves as an airy showcase for small items that the homeowner enjoys looking at.

LEFT Some built-ins are created purely for decorative purposes. This art niche shows off the homeowner's collection, with a painted back for contrast and interior lighting. LEDs are ideal for this purpose, as they won't add heat to delicate collectibles and require minimal energy to work.

Built-in cabinetry can also meet a bathroom's storage needs. In some cases, extra capacity is needed because of minimal space in a vanity. Other times, like here, a pedestal sink means no vanity storage is available and the built-in provides the room's only capacity.

freestanding furniture

● ● ● AS WE SPEND MORE TIME ENJOYING OUR bathrooms, rather than just rushing through our routines, the furniture we choose to include becomes more comfortable and stylish. This could be a plush vanity stool that makes makeup application more enjoyable. It could even be a chaise lounge or bistro table and chair for enjoying a cappuccino while the tub fills.

Side tables and garden stools have also become popular for holding cups, books, towels, or candles while bathing. There are also furniture pieces that double as storage, like armoires, freestanding cabinets, and small carts. Carts that let you roll them near a vanity or tub, depending on your need, can add an element of flexibility into your design.

LEFT A furniture piece can be an appealing stand-in for bulky cabinets, which can easily overwhelm a small room. An open etagere works well for towels and other visually appealing items. Less attractive necessities can be tucked into storage boxes or baskets that complement the room's style.

ABOVE A cart is ideal for holding small items near a vanity or tub. Wheels make it a mobile storage unit, which can be especially beneficial in a small bath where floor space is minimal and flexibility an asset.

ABOVE Some bathrooms are made for relaxation as well as hygiene. In those larger spaces, you'll often find furniture for the homeowner's comforts. These could be armchairs, ottomans, or chaises and side tables for tub essentials and luxuries.

LEFT A bench is a versatile piece of furniture that can serve as seating or as a side table (with tray). When used near a tub or shower, it's best to select water-friendly fabric for the ottoman's upholstery.

mirrors

●●● MIRRORS HELP US PRESENT OUR BEST look to the world, but they can also enhance the way our bathrooms look. You're not limited to the glued-on or clipped-on frameless sheet of glass your builder installed on the bathroom wall. Remodeling a bathroom or building a new one creates an ideal opportunity to explore the many style options available.

In most cases, you're going to have a mirror directly above your vanity area. Sometimes the mirror will be the facade of a medicine cabinet but if your medicine storage is positioned elsewhere, your mirror possibilities are limited only by your space, style preferences, and budget.

Framed mirrors are a popular option, and can be found at antique and salvage stores, art shops, hardware stores, home centers, or online. You may choose to have one custom-made from a professional framer, or purchase it from your cabinet source to match your vanity. Mirror glass can also be framed in the tile you use for your shower walls or wainscoting.

Mirrors are typically sized to match the vanity area, either as one large surface covering a dual sink countertop or as separate mirrors for each sink. It's important to factor in the mirror's frame projection if you're choosing a lighting fixture to go on the wall above it. You'll also want to factor in the frame width when determining its ideal placement above your countertop.

When one mirror extends across a dual sink area, lighting sconces are sometimes planned to install through the glass, with their wiring behind it. This takes careful coordination with your construction team, so that the lighting and mirror cuts end up at the right locations.

Full-length mirrors are also very helpful in a bathroom for getting dressed. These can be installed on a side wall with floor space in front of it, or on the back of a door, but be careful of weight limitations and anchoring with a hollow-core door installation.

BELOW A framed mirror from your cabinetry source is an easy choice. It will look good in the same space, may supply a shelf for small items, and provides style cohesion in a small bathroom.

FACING PAGE A framed mirror does not need to match the vanity below it. A well-chosen piece will complement the room and add a unique element of style and interest.

ABOVE If you're challenged by a wall of windows above your vanity, one increasingly popular solution is to install a simple mirror in front of the window. The tubular lights add flattering illumination to the natural light coming through the windows.

ABOVE One option for vanity mirrors is to frame them in tile that coordinates with the rest of the wall. This is usually done when a bathroom is being fully remodeled, but it can be done with a new tile installation and existing vanity, too.

RIGHT With larger mirrors, sconces are often located within their surface. This option requires careful coordination between designer, contractor, and the tradespeople handling each component of the project so that the connections and fixtures match up in the right location.

ABOVE While a framed mirror above each sink is a popular option, some homeowners opt for one shared mirror over both, as it provides a larger expanse of glass. This can additionally allow extra space for a TV between the sinks without affecting the full usability of either side.

LEFT In a heavily decorated space, simple works best. A frameless, beveled mirror lends charm with its shape but doesn't call attention away from the wall tile or sconces.

THE LED-ENHANCED MIRROR

light-emitting diodes, or LEDs, have become extremely popular for their low-energy illumination and versatility. They have also gotten so compact that they're turning up in mirrors. They may be designed as an illuminated frame, as a light fixture on top, as built-in side lights, or as an enhancement to a magnifying mirror. In states with strict energy codes, LED lighting in mirrors can add another layer of lighting without exceeding the allowances.

The lit frames are sometimes more useful as accent or night-lighting than as a task-lighting source on their own, though newer magnifying mirrors also employ LEDs to enhance tweezing and makeup application. Color is occasionally added as a dramatic accent; it may even be dimmable, changeable, or on a timed cycle, depending on your preference.

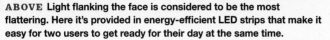

ABOVE Light flanking the face is considered to be the most flattering. Here it's provided in energy-efficient LED strips that make it easy for two users to get ready for their day at the same time.

RIGHT LEDs also are being used as a decorative element with color. Some are even designed to change color on a rotating basis, or at the user's request. Chromatherapy is popular with some as a way to relax or stimulate, depending on the chosen hue.

BELOW Magnifying mirrors are increasingly being added as a medicine cabinet accessory or vanity mirror insert for makeup application, eyebrow tweezing, and other close-up grooming. Incorporating LEDs into its frame makes those tasks even more efficient with added illumination.

ABOVE Lights above mirrors work well in many space-challenged installations. When you don't have room for side lights, an LED fixture built into the top of a mirror can add illumination with contemporary style.

installed accessories

● ● ● TOWEL BARS OR HOOKS, TOILET PAPER holders, robe hooks, tumbler and soap holders, built-in soap dispensers, and other installed elements can add style points, as well as functionality, to your bathroom. They're often chosen to coordinate with the styles and finishes of your faucets and cabinet hardware, but they can complement them instead of matching exactly.

The configurations you choose can add storage capacity to your bath. For example, a dual towel bar will hold two towels in the same space as one. Three or four hooks instead of a bar can increase your capacity even further, allowing robes to hang near the shower with your towels.

When planning your accessories, consider their location and hardware needs as well as their style. Will they need special screws to go into a tiled wall? Is there a light switch that would be blocked by a towel bar or hook? Is there a comfortably reachable spot near the toilet to hang the roll holder? If you're planning a glass or soap holder in your vanity area, how will it align with the mirror, backsplash, outlets, and other elements planned for that space? All of these questions need to be factored into your accessory planning before any construction work is done.

ABOVE A popular kitchen feature, the installed soap dispenser works well in a bathroom. It can both coordinate with the faucet selected and reduce countertop clutter. This is especially helpful in small bathrooms without much surface space.

RIGHT Rail systems, commonly used on kitchen backsplashes, can serve the same flexible organizing capacity in a bathroom. Each user can have a shelf to hold his or her personal items near where they'll be used.

•vanity and other accessories

Noninstalled accessories, on the other hand, can be chosen at your leisure, even after the bathroom is complete, if you prefer. They include tumblers, countertop soap dispensers, toothbrush holders, guest towel trays, cosmetics caddies, tissue box covers, and waste baskets. The ones you choose will depend on the room's purpose. A powder room, for example, does not generally need a toothbrush holder or cosmetic caddy, but will benefit from a guest towel tray, soap dispenser, tissue box cover, and wastebasket.

Children's bathrooms should always get nonbreakable accessories. Nonbreakable accessories are also beneficial for those with balance, depth perception, and other vision issues. Fortunately, today there are many attractive materials to choose from, especially resins and metals.

Accessories are easily replaced and donated to charity if your style preferences change over time, or if your children outgrow the cartoon character motif they once adored. Best of all, new ones can quickly and affordably enhance the look of your bathroom at any time.

ABOVE Accessories like soap dishes, tumblers, and other small, uninstalled pieces can add a fresh look to a bathroom without any work. Choose shapes, finishes, and materials that will work with what you have and how you live.

LEFT Vanity accessories can also be installed to keep work surfaces clear. Soap dispensers, as well as toothbrush and tumbler holders, can all be mounted on a wall. This is especially helpful if you have very limited countertop space, as many bathrooms do.

window treatments

●●● PRIVACY IS CRUCIAL IN BATHROOMS, SO your choice of window coverings becomes an important one. Light control may also be an issue, especially in suites where there is no door between the bedroom and bathroom.

You'll want to choose a style that works with the rest of the room or suite, but also be mindful of the covering's material. If the window is in the shower, it will need to be waterproof. If it's in a heavily used children's bathroom or a corner where you also wash your pets, it should be easy to clean, as well.

Formal window coverings, like drapery panels, are often selected for traditional master suites. It's common to use the same (or coordinating) coverings for both bedroom and bathroom. Formal drapery can also provide a dramatic backdrop to a focal point tub. If the coverings are meant to be permanently held back, you may still want a supplemental privacy option, perhaps in the form of a simple shade or blinds.

One option for bathroom window coverings is automation. These let you use a remote, wall switch, or smart phone connection to open or close the shades above a tub or high up in the shower, rather than have to strain to reach it. This is a great convenience for petite users, or anyone with accessibility challenges.

BELOW Fabric tapes add additional interest to window blinds. They can be a colorful accent or a complementary neutral. Either way, they upgrade the look over standard cord.

ABOVE Cellular shades provide privacy and temperature control. The bottom-up configuration allows privacy for someone relaxing in the tub while still letting in light from the top.

LEFT Layering is sometimes used for window coverings to provide light and privacy options. Though drapery panels are often a traditional choice, here they add contemporary style with their grommet tops and white-on-neutral pattern.

LEFT Opening and closing shades above wide or deep tubs can be awkward for many users. The remote control, which can be removed from its mount, makes this easy to do before getting into the bath.

Drapery panels can be used for privacy or decoration. Here they provide a stunning backdrop to the focal-point tub and draw your eye from the dramatic floor tile to the soaring arch.

more about...
WINDOW COVERINGS FOR WET AREAS

the most common waterproof window coverings are faux wood blinds or shutters. Both fit best with traditional and transitional decor. Production technology has made these faux woods nearly indistinguishable from their natural counterparts, but since they're made from composite materials, they don't warp or split even when drenched with shower spray.

It is possible to use water-resistant fabrics and a water-resistant rod to create a shower or tub-friendly window curtain. This is less frequently done in a shower stall, as the curtain may be pulled uncomfortably against the bather's skin, but it can be a nice option above a freestanding tub.

A modern bathroom would be better served with tinted glass or a tinted film or spray applied to the window, or with coverings built into the window itself. These are produced by manufacturers sandwiching blinds between interior and exterior panes of glass to create self-covered windows.

art and collectibles

●●● ART IS ALSO FINDING ITS WAY INTO THE bathroom. These pieces require extra care to avoid damage. Valuable collectibles should be protected from accidental falls by careful placement and, if recommended by an art dealer, secured to their location with a museum-grade adhesive. Storage niches or ledges can keep art objects out of busy work zones.

Paper- or canvas-based artworks should be framed by an experienced professional to protect them against moisture damage. Advise the framer that your piece will be placed in a full bathroom so that he or she takes extra precautions. Half baths don't need that extra level of care, as they're not subject to shower or tub steam. Sun damage, however, is always a consideration for art in rooms with direct sunlight, especially in those with an uncovered skylight.

A built-in niche will keep valuables out of the traffic flow, while showcasing them. Lighting and paint enhance their display, creating a museum effect in a master bath.

DISPLAYING ART AND COLLECTIBLES
IN YOUR BATHROOM

artwork and collectibles personalize your space, especially when they have sentimental value. It can be a collection of shells you acquired over years of family vacations, a grouping of photos of your wedding, or a prized painting by your favorite artist. Whatever the piece or pieces may be, you want to protect and enjoy them at the same time. Take any paper or canvas art works going into a bathroom where moisture may affect them to an experienced framer and let that professional know where they'll be hanging. Secure any breakable sculpture, glassware, or pottery with a museum adhesive or display on a shelf or niche that's out of reach.

Curate your collection. Rather than displaying an entire collection at once, choose a size-appropriate grouping for your space, so that it expresses your interest without overwhelming the room.

Choose a strategic location. If your collection requires shelf space, you'll want to place it where it won't be bumped during your morning and evening routines, but where you still can see it. This could be on a floating shelf mounted high on a side wall or in a built-in niche away from a busy traffic pattern. Larger items, like baskets or pottery, could be placed on a full-length shelf installed over the bathroom door.

Frame to complement. If your artwork is on paper, fabric, or canvas, you'll probably want to frame it. The framing elements can create a style statement on their own, but should always be chosen primarily to complement the artwork. Mats and frames should enhance, not overwhelm, the piece. They can also coordinate with other design elements in the room, but must work well with the artwork before anything else.

ABOVE Large items are often displayed on top of cabinetry. This keeps them out of the bathroom's work zones, but still easily visible. Breakable artworks may be secured with a museum-quality adhesive to avoid falling.

LEFT A favorite painting or photograph can beautifully enhance a bathroom, but it needs special care if the room has a tub or shower to protect against moisture damage. Powder rooms are the easiest to decorate with delicate artworks.

textiles

●●● THE TEXTILES YOU CHOOSE FOR YOUR bathroom can also reflect the room's style. Unlike installed elements, however, they are easy to change and update. There are offerings at every price level, with corresponding luxury and durability levels.

• bath mats and rugs

If your bathroom has a shower, tub, or both, you're probably going to want something soft to step out onto. You may also want something softer and warmer underfoot than your flooring material when standing barefoot at your vanity or visiting the toilet area.

You can now find bath mats that will extend across many double vanities or cover most of the floor of a standard secondary bathroom. This sometimes creates a better look for a small room than multiple mats.

• shower curtains

Shower curtains will definitely make a style statement in your bathroom. They can be playful and fun for a child's space or elegantly simple for a master bath. The rings that hold them on the rod, as well as the rod itself, should also tie into the style statement you're making and coordinate with the room's decor. An alternative to rings is a grommet style shower curtain. These are often selected for more casual or modern baths.

Many homeowners are opting for curved rods to create a roomier shower. Standard 72-inch-square shower curtains may be too narrow to cover them completely. Look for a curtain and liner that are about 12 inches wider.

ABOVE RIGHT The shower curtain and coordinating towels add a dash of orange zest to this neutral family bath. The dual mats let the eye rest with gray, while subtly playing with a pattern that complements the room's many squares. The overall effect is casual, pulled-together, and modern.

RIGHT The softly patterned botanical towels complement the room's geometrically patterned floor. Their muted tones lend sophisticated style to this quietly elegant space.

ABOVE A beautiful rug and vanity chair cover soften the hard lines of this modern bathroom. The rug also adds a gentle touch of color to the otherwise neutral palette. Before using a valuable rug in a full bathroom, consult a professional about its care and moisture tolerance.

LEFT Kids' bath towels don't have to carry a cartoon or superhero theme for them to appeal to lively young tastes. Choosing their favorite colors will make your investment more timeless. Complementing the white cabinetry and fixtures with ocean blue tones adds a beachy feel to this family bathroom.

ENHANCE YOUR BATH WITH
NEW ACCESSORIES

accessories are usually the last elements we choose for a room, but they can add—or subtract—quite a bit from its style. They are also instantly gratifying fixes—no tools necessary! Choose these finishing touches with as much care as you give the rest of the room's decor.

UPGRADE YOUR VANITY SET

Dated, damaged, or unsightly accessories can detract from your bathroom's appeal. Look for items that have become chipped or cracked, or whose materials don't reflect its style. These are easy to replace at your neighborhood home center, bath store, or favorite online site. You don't need to choose a matched set, but look for colors, textures, patterns, styles, and shapes that complement each other and the room.

SOFTEN YOUR LOOK

If your towels and bath rugs have become faded, stained, or worn, or don't look right with your room's new update, it's easy to replace them, too. These are best bought where you can feel the texture and see the colors in real life, but online purchases with a free return policy can work. You don't need to limit your rug choice to something made specifically for a bathroom either, but it should be water resistant and have a nonslip backing. If it doesn't, consider getting a nonslip pad to go under it.

ENHANCE YOUR VIEWS

If your mirror is not a glued- or clipped-on sheet of glass, you're in an excellent position to replace it yourself with something in a new style. (Glued-on mirrors need careful handling, and even oversize clipped-on mirrors can be difficult to handle.) You can also enhance your views with new artwork on the walls and new window coverings.

TOP A washable flokati rug adds a luxurious softness to the space. It can go in front of the vanity or the bathtub and shower for the homeowner's comfort. A rug backer will keep it in place.

ABOVE New mirrors will provide a dramatic facelift to the vanity wall, while still respecting its scale and color scheme.

LEFT A new vanity set will coordinate with the faucet's gold elements and the room's modernist approach, while providing a bit more contemporary style with its casual, organic shapes.

TIME FOR A REDO?

Updating your bathroom's accessories and decorative elements can give it a fresh new look. When remodeling doesn't make sense financially, this is another approach to getting a new look for a dated space.

photo credits

FRONT MATTER

p. ii-iii: Andrea Rugg Photography, design: West Bay Homes

p. 2-3: Adrian Van Anz, design: Dean Larkin, AIA/Dean Larkin Design/deanlarkindesign.com and Bradley Bayou/bradleybayou.com; Susan Teare Photography, design: Stephen Hart, Jennifer Lyford, Hart Associates Architects, Inc.; NanaWall Systems (left to right)

CHAPTER 1

p. 4: Brizo/www.brizo.com

p. 6: Ken Gutmaker, design: Paul Davis, AIA/Paul Davis Architects/pauldavisarchitects.com

p. 7: Susan Teare Photography (top left, bottom left), design: Jill S. Jarrett, CKD, CBD; Lauren Villano, AKBD/Jarrett Design LLC/www.jarrettdesignllc.com; Greg Riegler (right), design: Cheryl Kees Clendenon/In Detail Interiors/indetailinteriors.com

p. 8: Trent Bell Photography, design: Katahdin Cedar Log Homes

p. 9: Susan Teare Photography (top), design: Aparna Vijayan/Ulrich, Inc./www.ulrichinc.com; Ken Gutmaker (bottom), design: Jeffrey Hellmuth/JG Hellmuth Interior Design/JGHellmuth.com

p. 10: Trent Bell Photography, design: Whitten Architects

p. 11: Andrea Rugg Photography (left), design: Sylvestre Remodeling and Design; Andrea Rugg Photography (right), design: The New Old House Company

p. 12: Top Knobs/TopKnobs.com (top left); Daltile/Daltile.com (bottom left); Rev-A-Shelf LLC/www.rev-a-shelf.com (middle right); courtesy of Sherwin-Williams (bottom right)

p. 13: Susan Teare Photography, design: Joan Heaton Architects; builder: Brothers Building Company; stone: Burlington Marble and Granite

p. 14: Andrea Rugg Photography, design: Hendel Homes

p. 15: Andrea Rugg Photography, design: West Bay Homes

p. 16: Andrea Rugg Photography, design: Rosemary Merrill Design

p. 17: Andrea Rugg Photography (left), design: Sylvestre Remodeling and Design; Trent Bell Photography (right), design: Bowley Builders and Derek Preble

p. 18: Andrea Rugg Photography, design: West Bay Homes

p. 19: Susan Teare Photography (left), design: Julia Kleyman/Ulrich, Inc./www.ulrichinc.com; Susan Teare Photography (top right), design: Brad Rabinowitz Architect/bradrabinowitzarchitect.com and Red House Building/redhousebuilding.com; Andrea Rugg Photography (bottom right), design: Rosemary Merrill Design

p. 20: courtesy Kohler Co. (top left, bottom); California Faucets (top right)

p. 21: Susan Teare Photography, contractor: Alec Genung Construction

p. 22: John Tsantes (top), design: Cindy Grossmueller McClure & Jenna Randolph/Grossmueller's Design Consultants, Inc./www.grossmuellers.com; Ken Gutmaker (bottom), design: Tony Garcia, AIA/asquared studios/www.asquaredstudios.com

p. 23: Inalco/Tile of Spain Company/www.inalco.es/en (top); Andrea Rugg Photography (bottom), design: CF Design

p. 24: Tria Giovan

p. 25: Susan Teare Photography (top), contractor: Reap Construction, Richmond, VT; bench: Simpson Cabinetry, Essex, VT; Greg Riegler (bottom left, bottom right), design: Cheryl Kees Clendenon/In Detail Interiors/indetailinteriors.com

p. 26: Eric Roth, design: Elisa Allen

p. 27: Eric Roth, design: Peter Niemetz Design Group

p. 28: Matthew Millman Photography (left, right), design: Rachel Laxer Interiors/rlaxerinteriors.com

p. 29: Hulya Kolabas (top), design: Joanna Heimbold; Tria Giovan (bottom)

CHAPTER 2

p. 30: Susan Teare Photography, design: Aparna Vijayan/Ulrich, Inc./www.ulrichinc.com

pp. 32-33: courtesy of Inter Ikea Systems B.V./www.IKEA-USA.com (left); Susan Teare Photography (center), design: Sam Scofield Architect, AIA; builder: Peregrine Design Build; interior design: Kim Deetjen, principal at TruexCullins Architecture and Interior Design; Robern (top right); Lowe's/lowes.com (bottom right)

p. 34: Eric Roth, contractor: Shepard Construction, Weymouth, MA

p. 35: Eric Roth, design: Becky Finn

pp. 36-37: Jean Tuttle

pp. 38-39: courtesy Kohler Co.

p. 40: Susan Teare Photography, design: Peregrine Design Build/www.peregrinedesignbuild.com

p. 41: Andrea Rugg Photography, design: West Bay Homes

p. 42: Susan Teare Photography (left, right), design: Julia Kleyman/Ulrich, Inc./www.ulrichinc.com

p. 43: Susan Teare Photography, general contractor: Donald P. Blake Jr., Inc. and Travis Cutler; interior design: Marian Wright, Terri Gregory

p. 44: Tria Giovan

p. 45: Susan Teare Photography, design: Stephen Hart, Jennifer Lyford, Hart Associates Architects, Inc.

p. 46: Robern

p. 47: Delta Faucet (top); Brizo/www.brizo.com (bottom left); courtesy of TOTO/www.totousa.com (bottom right)

p. 48: Marlon DeCastro, design: Bonnie J. Lewis, Allied ASID, Assoc. IIDA, CAPS/55+ TLC Interior Design, LLC/55plustlc.com

p. 49: Ken Gutmaker, design: Anne Kellett, ASID, CAPS/A Kinder Space, San Diego, CA/akinderspace.com

p. 50: photo courtesy of Ginger®

p. 51: Delta Faucet (top); photo provided by Moen Incorporated/moen.com (bottom)

CHAPTER 3

p. 52: Tria Giovan

p. 54: Emily Followill Photography, design: Kandrac & Kole Interior Designs, Inc./www.Kandrac-Kole.com

p. 55: Aparici/Tile of Spain Company/www.aparici.com/en (top); Doyle Terry, design: Lance Stratton, Studio Stratton, Inc./www.studiostratton.com (bottom left); Tria Giovan (bottom right)

pp. 56-57: Susan Teare Photography (left), design: Mitra Samimi-Urich/Mitra Designs Studio Collaborative/mitradesigns.com; Ken Gutmaker (top right), design: Tony Garcia, AIA/asquared studios/www.asquaredstudios.com; photo © Duravit AG (bottom right)

p. 58: Ken Gutmaker (top), design: Jeffrey Hellmuth, JG Hellmuth Interior Design/JGHellmuth.com; Equipe Ceramicas/Tile of Spain Company/www.equipeceramicas.com/en (bottom)

p. 59: Jamie Gold, CKD, CAPS/Jamie Gold Kitchen and Bath Design/jgkitchens.com (top); Ryann Ford (bottom), design: Mell Lawrence Architects

p. 60: design: Realonda/Tile of Spain Company/www.realonda.com/en

p. 61: photo courtesy of Geberit

p. 62: Walker Zanger

p. 63: California Faucets (top); LINKASINK/www.linkasink.com (bottom left); Top Knobs/TopKnobs.com (bottom right)

p. 64: Ken Gutmaker (left), design: Anne Kellett, ASID, CAPS/A Kinder Space, San Diego, CA/akinderspace.com; Susan Teare Photography (right), design: Gregory C. Masefield Jr., AIA NCARB, Studio III Architecture, Bristol, VT/www.studio3architecture.net

p. 65: Ken Gutmaker, design: Jeffrey Hellmuth, JG Hellmuth Interior Design/JGHellmuth.com

p. 66: Lowe's/lowes.com (left); Charles Miller, courtesy *Fine Homebuilding* magazine, © The Taunton Press, Inc. (right)

p. 67: image provided by Bellacor.com representing Hudson Valley Lighting (top); Brizo/www.brizo.com (bottom left); Atlas Homewares/www.atlashomewares.com (bottom right)

p. 68: Ken Gutmaker, design: Jeffrey Hellmuth, JG Hellmuth Interior Design/JGHellmuth.com

p. 69: Mark Lohman, design: HAEFELE DESIGN

p. 70: Undine Prohl (left), design: Safdie Rabines Architects; Tria Giovan (right), design: Phillip Sides

p. 71: Susan Teare Photography, design: Stephen Hart, Hart Associates Architects, Inc.

CHAPTER 4

p. 72: Susan Teare Photography, general contractor: Patterson & Smith Construction—Shapleigh Smith, Chapman Smith; architectural design: Cushman Design Group—Milford Cushman, Ryan Beaulieu, Terri Gregory

p. 74: Inalco/Tile of Spain Company/www.inalco.es/en

p. 75: ROHL/www.rohlhome.com (top left); photo © Duravit AG (top right); courtesy Kohler Co. (bottom)

p. 76: Laufen Bathrooms AG/www.laufen.com (top); courtesy Kohler Co. (bottom)

p. 77: photo courtesy Native Trails by photographer Sean Sullivan (top); Susan Teare Photography (bottom left), design: Aparna Vijayan/Ulrich, Inc./www.ulrichinc.com; Thompson Traders/www.thompsontraders.com (bottom right)

p. 78: Brizo/www.brizo.com (top); ROHL/www.rohlhome.com (bottom)

p. 79: Trent Bell Photography for Leslie Saul & Associates

p. 80: Brizo/www.brizo.com (left); photo provided by Moen Incorporated/moen.com (right)

p. 81: Susan Teare Photography, design: Mitra Samimi-Urich/Mitra Designs Studio Collaborative/mitradesigns.com

p. 82: photo courtesy of Geberit (top); Greg Riegler (bottom), design: Cheryl Kees Clendenon/In Detail Interiors/indetailinteriors.com

p. 83: Kale Italia, a Ceramics of Italy brand/kaleitalia.com (top); Susan Teare Photography (bottom left), design: Mitra Samimi-Urich/Mitra Designs Studio Collaborative/mitradesigns.com; Susan Teare Photography (bottom right), design: Aparna Vijayan/Ulrich, Inc./www.ulrichinc.com

pp. 84-85: courtesy Kohler Co. (left, top right); courtesy of TOTO/www.totousa.com (center); Delta Faucet (bottom right)

p. 86: Susan Teare Photography, design: Aparna Vijayan/Ulrich, Inc./www.ulrichinc.com

p. 87: Tria Giovan (top); Chipper Hatter (bottom), design: Habify/www.habify.com

p. 88: courtesy Kohler Co. (left, right)

p. 89: courtesy Kohler Co.

p. 90: American Standard (left); Susan Teare Photography (right), design: Aparna Vijayan/Ulrich, Inc./www.ulrichinc.com

p. 91: photo courtesy Native Trails by photographer Sean Sullivan (top); Ryann Ford (bottom)

p. 92: Thompson Traders/www.thompsontraders.com (left); Azulev/Tile of Spain Company/www.azulevgrupo.com/en (right)

p. 93: American Standard (top); courtesy of Stone Forest, Inc./www.stoneforest.com (bottom)

p. 94: Susan Teare Photography (left), design: Aparna Vijayan/Ulrich, Inc./www.ulrichinc.com; Greg Riegler (right), design: Cheryl Kees Clendenon/In Detail Interiors/indetailinteriors.com

p. 95: Ken Gutmaker, design: Paul Davis, AIA/Paul Davis Architects/pauldavisarchitects.com

p. 96: Dune/Tile of Spain Company/www.dune.es/en

p. 97: photo provided by Moen Incorporated/moen.com (top left); Carolyn Bates (top right), design: Sandy Lawton; courtesy Kohler Co. (bottom)

p. 98: photo provided by Moen Incorporated/moen.com

p. 99: Delta Faucet (top); Chipper Hatter (bottom), design: Model Design, Inc./www.model-design.net

p. 100: courtesy *Fine Homebuilding* magazine, © The Taunton Press, Inc. (top left); courtesy Kohler Co. (top right, bottom)

p. 101: photo provided by Moen Incorporated/moen.com

CHAPTER 5

p. 102: William Lesch, design: Lori Carroll/Lori Carroll & Associates/loricarroll.com

p. 104: Susan Teare Photography (left), design: Stephen B. Jacobs Group, PC, Architect, and Andi Pepper Interior Design

p. 105: Susan Teare Photography (top left), design: Brad Rabinowitz Architect/bradrabinowitzarchitect.com and Red House Building/redhousebuilding.com; courtesy Kohler Co. (top right); Brizo/www.brizo.com (bottom)

pp. 106-107: Brizo/www.brizo.com (left); photo courtesy of Crossville, Inc. (top); Pfister, Inc. (bottom center); courtesy Kohler Co. (bottom right)

p. 108: Eric Roth, design: Butz and Klug Architects

p. 109: QuickDrain USA/www.quickdrainusa.com (left); California Faucets (top right and bottom right)

p. 110: Susan Teare Photography (left), design: Jill S. Jarrett, CKD, CBD; Lauren Villano, AKBD/Jarrett Design LLC/www.jarrettdesignllc.com; Brizo/www.brizo.com (right)

p. 111: Susan Teare Photography, design: Aparna Vijayan/Ulrich, Inc./www.ulrichinc.com

p. 112: ThermaSol (left); courtesy Kohler Co. (right)

p. 113: Ken Gutmaker, design: Paul Davis, AIA/Paul Davis Architects/pauldavisarchitects.com

p. 114: courtesy Kohler Co.

p. 115: Walker Zanger (top left); ROHL/www.rohlhome.com (bottom left); courtesy Kohler Co. (right)

p. 116: photo courtesy of Crossville, Inc. (left); Ken Gutmaker (right), design: Paul Davis, AIA/Paul Davis Architects/pauldavisarchitects.com

p. 117: Susan Teare Photography (left), design: Brad Rabinowitz Architect/bradrabinowitzarchitect.com and Red House Building/redhousebuilding.com; Walker Zanger (right)

p. 118: Susan Teare Photography, design: Mitra Samimi-Urich/Mitra Designs Studio Collaborative/mitradesigns.com

p. 119: ThermaSol (left); Tria Giovan (top), design: Jennifer Vreeland, JV Design Style

p. 120: photo provided by Moen Incorporated/moen.com (right)

p. 121: photo provided by Moen Incorporated/moen.com (top); Grohe (bottom)

p. 122: Susan Teare Photography (left), design: Aparna Vijayan/Ulrich, Inc./www.ulrichinc.com; Susan Teare Photography (right), design: Jill S. Jarrett, CKD, CBD; Lauren Villano, AKBD/Jarrett Design LLC/www.jarrettdesignllc.com

p. 123: Tucker English, courtesy *Fine Homebuilding* magazine, © The Taunton Press, Inc.

p. 124: Hansgrohe/www.hansgrohe-usa.com (left); Brandon A. Smith (right), design: Marlaina Teich/Marlaina Teich Designs

p. 125: Tria Giovan

CHAPTER 6

p. 126: Ken Gutmaker, design: Tony Garcia, AIA/asquared studios /www.asquaredstudios.com

p. 128: courtesy of Inter Ikea Systems B.V./www.IKEA-USA.com

p. 129: Brandon A. Smith (top), design: Betsy Burnham & Max Humphrey/Burnham Design; Brandon A. Smith (bottom), Gail Sedigh/AFK Fine Furniture for Children

p. 130: bath by Knocknock kitchen and bath design/www.knocknocksite.com

p. 131: Lowe's/lowes.com (left); Susan Teare Photography (right), design: Brad Rabinowitz Architect/bradrabinowitzarchitect.com *and* Red House Building/redhousebuilding.com

p. 132: Atlas Homewares/www.atlashomewares.com

p. 133: courtesy of Inter Ikea Systems B.V./www.IKEA-USA.com (top); Atlas Homewares/www.atlashomewares.com (bottom left, bottom right)

p. 134: Atlas Homewares/www.atlashomewares.com (left); Woodworkers Source (right)

p. 135: Charles Miller, courtesy *Fine Homebuilding* magazine, © The Taunton Press, Inc. (left); Benjamin Moore & Co./benjaminmoore.com (top right); © Showplace Cabinetry/www.ShowplaceWood.com (bottom right)

p. 136: Robern

p. 137: Susan Teare Photography (left), design: Julia Kleyman/Ulrich, Inc./www.ulrichinc.com; courtesy of Hastings Tile & Bath, Inc./www.hastingstilebath.com (right)

p. 138: Robern (top, bottom)

p. 139: Robern (left); © Duravit AG (right)

p. 140: Ken Gutmaker, design: Tony Garcia, AIA/asquared studios/www.asquaredstudios.com

p. 141: Ken Gutmaker (top left), design: Paul Davis, AIA/Paul Davis Architects/pauldavisarchitects.com; courtesy of Inter Ikea Systems B.V./www.IKEA-USA.com (top right); Greg Riegler (bottom), design: Cheryl Kees Clendenon/In Detail Interiors/indetailinteriors.com

p. 142: Rev-A-Shelf LLC/www.rev-a-shelf.com (top left); © Duravit AG (top right); photo courtesy of Kraftmaid Cabinetry/www.Kraftmaid.com (bottom)

p. 143: courtesy Kohler Co. (top); Rev-A-Shelf LLC/www.rev-a-shelf.com (bottom)

p. 144: Wilsonart/wilsonart.com

p. 145: Jamie Gold, CKD, CAPS /Jamie Gold Kitchen and Bath Design/jgkitchens.com (top left); Neolith/Tile of Spain Company/www.neolith.com (top right); Wilsonart/wilsonart.com (bottom)

p. 146: Chipper Hatter (top), design: Countertop Shoppe; William Lesch, design: Lori Carroll/Lori Carroll & Associates/loricarroll.com (bottom)

p. 147: Wilsonart/wilsonart.com

CHAPTER 7

p. 148: Ken Gutmaker, design: Paul Davis, AIA/Paul Davis Architects/pauldavisarchitects.com

p. 150: Lowe's/lowes.com

p. 151: Eric Roth (left), design: Leslie Fine Interiors; Cali Bamboo (right)

p. 152: Inalco/Tile of Spain Company/www.inalco.es/en

p. 153: Vives/Tile of Spain Company/www.vivesceramica.com (top); Tria Giovan (bottom)

p. 154: Jamie Gold, CKD, CAPS/Jamie Gold Kitchen and Bath Design/jgkitchens.com and Terry Smith, CMKBD, CAPS/TS Cabinetry and Design/terrysmithdesign.com

p. 155: Undine Prohl, design: Dry Design

p. 156: John Tsantes (left), design: Cindy Grossmueller McClure & Jenna Randolph/Grossmueller's Design Consultants, Inc./www.grossmuellers.com; Susan Teare Photography (right), design: Jill S. Jarrett, CKD, CBD; Lauren Villano, AKBD/Jarrett Design LLC/www.jarrettdesignllc.com

p. 157: Adrian Van Anz, design: Dean Larkin, AIA/Dean Larkin Design/deanlarkindesign.com and Bradley Bayou/bradleybayou.com

pp. 158-159: Realonda/Tile of Spain Company/www.realonda.com/en (left); Lunada Bay Tile (top center); Atlas Concorde, a Ceramics of Italy brand, atlasconcorde.com (bottom center); Walker Zanger (right)

p. 160: Porcelanosa/Tile of Spain Company/www.porcelanosa-usa.com

p. 161: Levantina/Tile of Spain Company/www.levantina.com/us/ (top left); courtesy of Crossville, Inc. (top right); Florim, a Ceramics of Italy brand, florim.it (bottom)

p. 162: Adrian Van Anz, design: Dean Larkin, AIA/Dean Larkin Design/deanlarkindesign.com and Bradley Bayou/bradleybayou.com

p. 163: courtesy Kohler Co. (top left); Emily Followill Photography (bottom left), design: Kandrac & Kole Interior Designs, Inc./www.Kandrac-Kole.com; courtesy of ANN SACKS (right) pp. 164-165: Charles Miller, courtesy *Fine Homebuilding* magazine, © The Taunton Press, Inc. (left); Made Goods (top right); Benjamin Moore & Co./benjaminmoore.com (bottom center); Walker Zanger (bottom right)

p. 166: Tria Giovan

p. 167: Jeremy Swanson (top left), design: Anne H. Grice/Anne Grice Interiors/ www.annegrice.com; Ken Gutmaker (top right), design: Paul Davis, AIA/Paul Davis Architects/pauldavisarchitects.com; NanaWall Systems (bottom)

p. 168: Lowe's/lowes.com

p. 169: NanaWall Systems (top); Andersen Windows/www.andersenwindows.com (bottom left); Ken Gutmaker (bottom right), design: Paul Davis, AIA/Paul Davis Architects/pauldavisarchitects.com

CHAPTER 8

p. 170: Mark Lohman, design: Caroline Burke Designs

p. 172: Robern (top); © Duravit AG (bottom)

p. 173: Imola Ceramica, a Ceramics of Italy brand, imolaceramica.com (top); ODL Tubular Skylights/www.odltubularskylights.com (bottom left); Brizo/www.brizo.com (bottom right)

pp. 174-175: Lowe's/lowes.com (left); courtesy of Sea Gull Lighting (center); Corbett Lighting, courtesy of Paul Finkel (top right); Jeff Schlicht (bottom right), design: Victor Sun, Designer/KE Design Studio/ kedesignstudios.com

p. 176: courtesy Kohler Co. (left); Hudson Valley Lighting (top right); Pegasus Lighting/ www.pegasuslighting.com (bottom right)

p. 177: courtesy Kohler Co.

p. 178: Warmup

p. 179: Susan Teare Photography (left), design: Jill S. Jarrett, CKD, CBD; Lauren Villano, AKBD/Jarrett Design LLC/www. jarrettdesignllc.com; ThermaSol (right)

p. 180: Susan Teare Photography (left), general contractor: Donald P. Blake Jr., Inc. and Travis Cutler; architectural design: Cushman Design Group—Milford Cushman and Chad Forcier, interior design: SATA Interior Design--Sara Tauben; Greg Riegler (right), design: Cheryl Kees Clendenon/In Detail Interiors/indetailinteriors.com

p. 181: Susan Teare Photography, general contractor: Donald P. Blake Jr. Inc. and Travis Cutler; architectural design: Cushman Design Group—Milford Cushman and Kelley Osgood; interior design: Marian Wright and Terry Gregory

p. 182: Broan-NuTone, LLC (left, right)

p. 183: Susan Teare Photography, design: Gregory C. Masefield Jr. AIA NCARB, Studio III Architecture/www.studio3architecture.net

CHAPTER 9

p. 184: Carolyn Bates, design: Haynes & Garthwaite Architects

pp. 186-187: Lutron Electronics Co., Inc. (left, top); courtesy Kohler Co (bottom center); LookinGlass Mirrored TV/www. lookinglasstv.com (right)

p. 188: Lutron Electronics Co., Inc.

p. 189: Renovisions (top); LookinGlass Mirrored TV/www.lookinglasstv.com (bottom)

pp. 190-191: © Docking Drawer/www. dockingdrawer.com (left); Brian Pontolilo, courtesy *Fine Homebuilding* magazine, © The Taunton Press, Inc. (center); Lutron Electronics Co., Inc. (top right, bottom right)

CHAPTER 10

p. 192: Susan Teare Photography, general contractor: Tom Herrington, architect: John Lederer, interior design: Cushman Design Group—Milford Cushman, Kelley Osgood, Chad Forcier, Terri Gregory

p. 194: Greg Riegler (left), design: Cheryl Kees Clendenon/In Detail Interiors/ indetailinteriors.com; Susan Teare Photography (right), design: Mitra Samimi-Urich/Mitra Designs Studio Collaborative/ mitradesigns.com

p. 195: Susan Teare Photography, design: Julia Kleyman/Ulrich, Inc./www.ulrichinc.com

p. 196: Brandon A. Smith (left), design: Christopher Kennedy/Christopher Kennedy, Inc.; courtesy of Inter Ikea Systems B.V./ www.IKEA-USA.com (right)

p. 197: Grohe (top); bathroom courtesy of Decora Cabinets/decoracabinets.com (bottom)

p. 198: Lowe's/lowes.com (left); Greg Riegler (right), design: Cheryl Kees Clendenon/In Detail Interiors/indetailinteriors.com

p. 199: Randall Perry Photography, design: Balzer + Tuck Architecture and Leah Margolis Design, LLC

p. 200: Mark Lohman (left), design: Haefele Design; Susan Teare Photography (right), architects: Mark Bromley & Ben Bush, Hillview Design Collaborative, and Jim Sanford, Sanford/Strauss Architects; builder: Leach Construction of Vermont; designer: Casey Blanchard

p. 201: Susan Teare Photography (top), design: Stephen Hart, Hart Associates Architects, Inc.; general contractor: Gilman Guidelli & Bellow; interior design: Paula Callanan, Nicole Goldman; Greg Riegler (bottom), design: Cheryl Kees Clendenon/In Detail Interiors/indetailinteriors.com

pp. 202-203: Robern (left); courtesy of Hastings Tile & Bath, Inc./www.hastingsbath. com (center); Robern (top right); © Duravit AG (bottom right)

p. 204: Pfister, Inc. (left); courtesy of Inter Ikea Systems B.V./www.IKEA-USA.com (right)

p. 205: courtesy of Inter Ikea Systems B.V./ www.IKEA-USA.com (top, bottom)

p. 206: Smith & Noble/smithandnoble.com (left, center, right)

p. 207: Smith & Noble/smithandnoble.com (top); Walker Zanger (bottom)

p. 208: Susan Teare Photography, design: Mitra Samimi-Urich/Mitra Designs Studio Collaborative/mitradesigns.com

p. 209: Brandon A. Smith (left), design: Marlaina Teich/Marlaina Teich Designs; Susan Teare Photography (right), design: Jill S. Jarrett, CKD, CBD; Lauren Villano, AKBD/ Jarrett Design LLC/www.jarrettdesignllc.com

p. 210: courtesy of Inter Ikea Systems B.V./ www.IKEA-USA.com (top); Doyle Terry (bottom), design: Lance Stratton, Studio Stratton, Inc./www.studiostratton.com

p. 211: Fred Licht (top), design: Stephan Jones/Stephan Jones Interiors/stephanjones. com; courtesy of Inter Ikea Systems B.V./ www.IKEA-USA.com (bottom)

p. 212: www.jcpenney.com (left); Shades of Light (top right, bottom right)

p. 213: courtesy Kohler Co.